Keith Haring, Andy Warhol, and Walt Disney

Organized by the Phoenix Art Museum
Bruce D. Kurtz, Curator of Twentieth-Century Art

Supported by Phelps Dodge Corporation
and COMPAS (Combined Metropolitan Phoenix Arts
and Sciences)

Phoenix Art Museum
Phoenix, Arizona   March 23 – May 12, 1991

Tacoma Art Museum
Tacoma, Washington   February 14 – March 29, 1992

Corcoran Gallery of Art
Washington D.C.   June 3 – August 15, 1992

Worcester Art Museum
Worcester, Massachusetts
September 19 – December 6, 1992

Keith Haring, Andy Warhol, and Walt Disney

Edited by Bruce D. Kurtz

With contributions by
Bruce Hamilton and Geoffrey Blum, Dave Hickey,
and Bruce D. Kurtz

Phoenix Art Museum

Prestel

Published in conjunction with the exhibition of the same name,
organized by the Phoenix Art Museum and shown there from March 23 – May 12, 1991.

Exhibition itinerary:
Tacoma Art Museum, Tacoma, Washington (February 14 – March 29, 1992)
Corcoran Gallery of Art, Washington D.C. (June 3 – August 15, 1992)
Worcester Art Museum, Worcester, Massachusetts (September 19 – December 6, 1992)

Text editor: Moira Banks

Frontispiece: Andy Warhol, *The Marx Brothers* from the portfolio
Ten Portraits of Jews of the Twentieth Century, 1980 (catalogue number 96)

Prestel-Verlag, Mandlstrasse 26, D-8000 Munich 4, Germany
Tel: (89) 38 17 09 0; Fax: (89) 38 17 09 35

Distributed in continental Europe by Prestel-Verlag
Verlegerdienst München GmbH & Co KG
Gutenbergstrasse 1, D-8031 Gilching, Germany, Tel: (81 05) 21 10; Fax: (81 05) 55 20

Distributed in the USA and Canada by te Neues Publishing Company,
15 East 76th Street, New York, NY 10021, USA
Tel: (212) 288 0265; Fax: (212) 570 2373

Distributed in Japan by YOHAN-Western Publications Distribution
Agency, 14-9 Okubo 3-chome, Shinjuku-ku, J-Tokyo 169
Tel: (3) 208 0181; Fax: (3) 209 0288

Distributed in the United Kingdom, Ireland and all remaining
countries by Thames & Hudson Limited, 30-34 Bloomsbury Street, London WC1B 3 QP, England
Tel: (71) 636 5488; Fax: (71) 636 4799

Designed by Dietmar Rautner
Typeset by Max Vornehm, Munich
Color separations by Gewa-Repro GmbH, Gerlinger und Wagner, Munich
Printed and bound by Passavia Druckerei GmbH, Passau
Printed in Germany
ISBN 3-7913-1146-8

Contents

Foreword

Keith Haring was a good friend to me and to the Phoenix Art Museum. I first met him in 1985 when I asked him to design a banner, billboard, and T-shirt for an exhibition titled *American Art of the 1980s: Selections from the Eli and Edythe L. Broad Collection* at the Phoenix Art Museum. (The billboard drawing is catalogue number 127.) Keith's dealer, Tony Shafrazi, took me to Keith's New York studio where he agreed to donate his art to the project and expressed interest in coming to Phoenix. It was the first of many occa-sions when I was struck by his generosity, open-ness, and sincerity. I felt an instant rapport with him.

Haring visited Phoenix for six days in December 1986, giving a drawing workshop for 250 people at the museum, a lecture about his art to a crowd of 350, at least a dozen interviews, collaborating with 25 high school students on a 11 x 160-foot mural (see pages 152 and 153), making several editions of prints, and finding the time and energy to party, too. His energy was extraordinary.

One anecdote will illustrate the effect he had on people. A Mexican restaurant in the barrio was his favorite place to eat, and each time we went there another newspaper article, radio program, or tele-vision appearance had taken place, so every time the hostess, waitresses, and cook warmed to Keith a little more. He could communicate so personally through the media that thousands of people grew to feel that they got to know him, and many of them actually did.

During Keith's Phoenix visit he met with the Phoenix Art Commission's Public Art Committee to discuss designing a playground for a city park. One of my many regrets that Keith died so young is that the playground was never designed.

On the last night of Keith's visit to Phoenix I gave a party in his honor in a high-rise apartment I wanted to buy but for which I did not yet have a contract or a loan. The seller was persuaded to let me have the party by the offer of Keith making him a small drawing as a thank you, which he graciously did, along with one for me.

The apartment had no furniture in it, and the elec-tricity had not been turned on, but we had valet parking. We filled up the bathtub with ice and eight cases of bottled beer, set up candles, glow sticks, and road emergency lights all around, had bags and boxes of munchies, and Keith was the DJ on a battery-operated boom box. About 125 people showed up. We had so much fun that Keith talked about it almost every time I saw him after that. There is still a small burn on the living room car-pet that I did not remove because it is a souvenir of the party.

After that, I saw Keith nearly every time I was in New York. We went together to the opening of the new Twentieth-Century Art wing at the Metropoli-tan Museum of Art, meeting at the National Arts Club where Keith's friend Louise Bourgeois was receiving an honor that evening. Keith looked smashing in his green and black patterned silk tuxedo. The photographers followed him through the first three galleries of the Met's new wing until he waved them away, and at the end of our circuit CBS News interviewed him. He was always polite and cooperative with the media, even when he would have preferred not to be bothered.

From the time we first met we talked about doing a show together. Tony Shafrazi did not want the Phoenix Art Museum to organize a survey of Keith's work because he felt it would preclude the Whitney or MoMA from doing it until several years later (not that they had any plans then). So we decided to do a small show of Keith's drawings for posters, watches, T-shirts, billboards, and other objects, along with the objects that were made from the drawings. It was when we were working on this project that he mentioned that Andy War-hol and Walt Disney were his heroes, and I asked how he would feel about our organizing a show of

all three artists. "Fantastic," he said. But he died before we could do it together.

So the current exhibition became a tribute to a dead friend. I think Keith would have been happy with the show. I'm sorry he never got to see it.

I met with Andy Warhol several times, but did not know him as well as I knew Keith. In 1966 I made my first trip to New York as a graduate student and went to Warhol's first "Factory," as he called his studio. He was my hero then. The Factory was at 231 East Forty-Seventh Street in an old firehouse. The elevator was painted silver with "The Factory" hand-lettered in black next to the correct button to push. I just walked into the legendary silver-painted and aluminum-foil-covered studio, as anybody could have then. Andy was not there but his assistant, Gerard Melanga, was, so I talked to him for awhile and hung out a little. We struck up a friendship that lasted for several years.

Gerard and I saw each other again after Andy moved The Factory to Union Square in 1968, and that time I met Warhol. Over the course of several years and visits, Andy introduced me to some of The Factory regulars, like Jackie Curtis, Holly Woodlawn, Joe Dallesandro, Paul Morrisey, Brigid Polk, and others whose names I don't remember. Andy always im-pressed me by how quiet, shy, and extremely polite he was, and in that he would say some of the most mundane things that came out sounding brilliant, like his art.

The first exhibition I organized was of Andy Warhol prints in 1969, for Hartwick College in Upstate New York where I taught. We had the *Campbell's Soup Cans,* the *Marilyns,* the *Flowers,* the *Kennedy Assassination* portfolio, and a few others. The college's president was so outraged by the soup cans that he asked me to take them down, but I refused. In 1970 Gerard came to screen Warhol's films *Vinyl* and *Chelsea Girls,* which caused both rapture and havoc. Students still tell me what a momentous event seeing Warhol's films was for them. When

the faculty later debated whether or not to initiate co-ed dormitories, a German professor said that doing so would result in something like the *Chelsea Girls,* then proceeded to describe every lurid scene. (The faculty voted in favor of the proposal.) The last time I saw Warhol was in 1981 at his studio at 860 Broadway, in the old S + H Green Stamp offices, when I was writing an essay for *Artforum* about Max's Kansas City, the legendary bar/restaurant Mickey Ruskin ran near Union Square where Warhol and his crowd held court in the back room at the round table. Max's was a great meeting place for film-makers, dancers, painters, sculptors, poets, actors, and all kinds of creative people. Mickey created an atmosphere where anything was allowed.

On one night Cary Grant and Judy Garland might be there along with the King and Queen of Thailand, a fashion model with a baby elephant, Jane Fonda, Robert Smithson, Candy Darling, Tennessee Williams, Carl Andre, Jim Morrison, Janis Joplin, Eric Emerson, Andrea Feldman, and Alice Cooper. In his book *POPism: the Warhol '60s,* Warhol said that Max's "was the exact place where Pop Art and pop life came together in New York in the '60s."[1] I spoke with Warhol briefly about Max's for my essay, but mostly I talked with Brigid Polk. And then Warhol died before I got to see him again. While the exhibition started with the idea that Warhol and Disney were Haring's two heroes, later I realized that Warhol and Haring were two of mine. I never met Disney, but who hasn't been to Disneyland or seen dozens of his films? Let me also point out that, while the exhibition is titled *Keith Haring, Andy Warhol, and Walt Disney,* the essays in this catalogue intentionally appear in the opposite order to indicate a chronological development beginning with Disney, the oldest of these artists, and progressing to Warhol, then Haring.

Though the exhibition has a lot of personal meaning for me, many other people worked together to

make it possible. First and foremost was Keith Haring. The Phelps Dodge Company and COMPAS (Combined Metropolitan Phoenix Arts and Sciences) generously supported the exhibition with funds. The many individuals and institutions whose names appear on page 10 kindly lent their artworks. Dave Hickey and Bruce Hamilton wrote incisive essays that contribute their perceptions to our catalogue. Staff members of the Estate of Keith Haring were immensely helpful and cooperative, including Julia Gruen, Keith's assistant since 1984; Margaret Slabbert, Keith's financial manager since 1987; and David Stark. They assis-ted at every step in this complicated project. From the Walt Disney Company, Kay Salz in the animation library se-lected the artworks for Disney to lend and tire-lessly provided information throughout the pro-ject, and Esther Ewert and Anna Cole steered our request for copyright permissions through the many channels. They were extremely supportive. At the Andy Warhol Foundation for the Visual Arts, Inc., New York, Vincent Freemont, Pamela Clapp, Donna De Salvo, and Jane Rubin assisted with loans of artworks, information, and copy-right permissions. We are grateful for their help.

The entire staff of the Phoenix Art Museum par-ticipated in the exhibition in one way or another, but I would like to single out a few people who made especially significant contributions. First on the list is the museum's director, Jim Ballinger, who endorsed the idea of the exhibition the moment I mentioned it and supported with enthu-siasm and the necessary resources all of our efforts to organize and tour the show and prepare the catalogue. Ingenious special promotional efforts were made by Gail Griffin and Margaret Fries, including bus shelter posters, a banner, promotio-nal posters, and a flyer stating "Get Your Can to the Phoenix Art Museum" that was distributed in supermarkets and gave admission to the museum for a can of Campbell's Soup. The 8,000 cans of soup we collect-ed were given to the Saint Mary's Food Bank for distribution to the needy. The education depart-ment's Margaret Maynard and Jan Krulick devised a much-used children's activities area, a children's *Look Book* with projects for them to complete in the exhibition and take home, a tunnel entrance for kids, a free admission "Color Me and Be Free" flyer, and a "Heroes' Wall" depict-ing heroes of the education department's youth group, Teen Arts Council for Educational Enrichment, or TACKEE. The museum's talented Chief Preparator and Exhibition Designer, David Restad, designed and built, along with Gene Koeneman and Bob Gates, a beautiful installation that Keith would have loved (page 23), including the tunnel entrance, a video room, and the children's activities area that the education department conceived and David made concrete. The museum's Registrar, Heather Northway, and her assistant Brenda Rayman made all of the complicated shipping arrangements for the nearly 200 artworks in the show, both to assemble the show and to tour it, keeping track of the locations of each object every step of the way. Suzanne Gaynor, Cathy Lemon, Genni Houlihan, and Craig Smith were meticulous in attending to the photography that was needed for the catalogue and for the essayists and venues. Karen Hodges ably assisted with many administrative details while I was writing the catalogue. Adrienne Whi-taker, an undergraduate intern from Arizona State University, prepared the biographies and biblio-graphies and provided research assistance. And last but not least, Janet Hillson prepared the numerous drafts of the checklist and performed countless other supportive tasks throughout the whole project, not to mention the moral support that she and all the others provided. This exhibi-tion and catalogue are truly group projects for which the people named above deserve a great deal of the credit.

Lenders to the Exhibition

Mr. and Mrs. Harry W. Anderson, Atherton, California
Martin and Janet Blinder, Los Angeles, California
Mr. and Mrs. William H. Bonifas, Milwaukee, Wisconsin
Mr. and Mrs. Kerby Confer, Augusta, Georgia
The Walt Disney Company, Burbank, California
Ronald Feldman Fine Arts, Inc., New York, New York
Mr. George F. Getz, Jr., Scottsdale, Arizona
Mr. and Mrs. Bruce Hamilton, Prescott, Arizona
The Estate of Keith Haring, New York, New York
Jan and Bill Kenyon, Phoenix, Arizona
Margo Leavin Gallery, Los Angeles, California
Los Angeles County Museum of Art, Los Angeles, California
Martin Lawrence Limited Editions, Van Nuys, California
The Robert B. Mayer Memorial Loan Collection, Chicago, Illinois
Robert Miller Gallery, Inc., New York, New York
Phoenix Art Museum, Phoenix, Arizona
The Security Pacific Corporation, Los Angeles, California
Editions Shellman, Munich, Germany, and New York, New York
Andrew Sie, Maitland, Florida
University Art Museum, University of New Mexico, Albuquerque, New Mexico
The Andy Warhol Foundation for the Visual Arts, Inc., New York, New York
Frederick R. Weisman Art Foundation, Los Angeles, California

Keith Haring, Andy Warhol, and Walt Disney

by Bruce D. Kurtz

The Most Popular Artists Walt Disney, Andy Warhol, and Keith Haring are among the most popular artists America has ever produced. The oldest of the three, Disney (1901–1966), created an entertainment empire featuring Mickey Mouse and Donald Duck that became the ultimate example of popular art's mass appeal.

Warhol (1928–1987) was the first fine artist to utilize the icon-making effects of mass media in his art. His aphorism that "In the future, everyone will be world famous for fifteen minutes" has often been quoted by presidents and movie stars.[1] Warhol's incursion into the formerly dubious aesthetic territory of mass media icons gave license to the next generation, represented by Keith Haring (1958–1990).

Haring's earliest work that gained wide attention – his chalk drawings on the black paper that had been pasted over expired advertising posters in New York City subways – imitated advertising's context and addressed the mass media's populist audience. Throughout his career Haring made images that were as comprehensible as cartoons and MTV. Each artist had an uncanny ability to feel artistically the pulse of American popular culture. At the same time, each helped to create it.

The idea for this exhibition came from a conversation with Keith Haring when we were working on an exhibition of his art and he said that Warhol and Disney were his two heroes. Later I discovered that Trevor Fairbrother had asked Andy Warhol, "Who in history would you choose to paint you?" and Warhol replied, "Walt Disney. He'd make me look like a duck."[2]

Both Warhol and Haring made images of Disney's most famous creation, Mickey Mouse (catalogue numbers 98, 106 and 119). Haring's many drawings, paintings, and prints of *Andy Mouse* (catalogue numbers 126, 130–33 and 140) superimpose Warhol's face on Mickey Mouse's body, graphically representing Haring's admiration for the two older artists. Regarding Haring's drawing *Money Magazine "Andy Mouse Bill"* (catalogue number 133), the artist said "It's like treating him [Warhol] like he was part of American culture, like Mickey Mouse was. That he himself had become a symbol, a sign for something completely, universally understandable. He sort of made this niche for himself in the culture. As much as Mickey Mouse had ... putting him on a dollar bill was just making him even more like an icon or part of the American dream."[3]

Walt Disney's Mickey Mouse represents how Americans would like to perceive themselves. The American author John Updike observed that: "The America that is not symbolized by that imperial Yankee Uncle Sam is symbolized by Mickey Mouse. He is America as it feels to itself – plucky, put-on, inventive, resilient, good-natured, game."[4] He is also proletarian, playing roles like a teamster, taxi driver, castaway, fisherman, jockey, storekeeper, sailor, convict, fireman, and gaucho.

Disney's achievement of objectifying America's national character fantasy in the easy to understand and likeable Mickey Mouse must have struck the son of a Czech laborer, Andy Warhol, both as a phenomenal characterization and as a great career move. Peter Schjeldahl wrote that "Warhol is one of the very, very few modern artists from an authentically working-class background.... For the most part, the American working class in our time has been characterized by avidity for the products and values of capitalist popular culture; ambivalence about these things usually has been the province of a middle class able to take their availability for granted from birth."[5]

"Avidity for the products of popular culture" is the

central feature of Warhol's art. That Disney created the most pervasive cartoon character in the world and built a massive entertainment empire upon it inspired Warhol, with empire-building ambitions of his own in painting, printmaking, photography, films, and publishing.

Disney died in 1966 without having met either Warhol or Haring, but the latter two artists knew each other well. They talked at least weekly from the time they met in 1983 until Warhol's death in 1987. When other artists advised Haring against it, Warhol encouraged him to open the Pop Shop in 1986 – a store selling Haring-designed items like buttons, T-shirts (catalogue number 195), posters, a radio, inflatable baby, Swatch watches, refrigerator magnets, and other consumer goods. Haring wanted his art, like Disney's, to be available to a large audience that could not afford the high cost of paintings. That Haring took Warhol's advice more seriously than that of other artists confirms the younger artist's admiration. Warhol's and Haring's mutual respect extended to collaborating on a painting of Madonna for a wedding gift when she married Sean Penn (page 20).

While Haring and Warhol paid homage to Mickey Mouse's iconic status and admired Disney as an artistic role model, Disney was not influenced by either artist. However, the three artists share several characteristics: they all collaborated with other artists, used mass media as integral parts of their art, used mass production to make quantities of their images, and took great interest in entertainers and entertainment.

Collaboration with Other Artists A single Walt Disney animated film requires many artists collaborating together. The collaboration begins when writers prepare a story treatment which the "concept artists" then translate into "inspirational" sketches and paintings defining the characters' design and personalities. The "inspirational" images also suggest the mood, lighting, color scheme, and time of day (catalogue number 13). The director, story writers, and story sketch artists then use the concept art to develop storyboards showing possible film sequences.

Following the sound recordings of the voice artists, animators produce rough pencil drawings which show "extremes" – the furthest points of movement for a given action (catalogue numbers 18–26, 36–41, and 54–59). Assistant animators, "breakdown" and "in-between" crews then develop intermediate poses. "Clean-up" artists re-draw the series, refining proportion and detail (catalogue numbers 73–76).

Inkers and painters next transfer the animation drawings onto clear acetate sheets called "cels,"[6] filling in the colors of the characters and inking in the special effects by hand. Animation drawings were hand traced onto cels using colored inks before 1960, but since then the drawings have been reproduced directly onto cels through a special Xerox process which retains the animators' spontaneity and eliminates time-consuming tracing.

The clear acetate cels with characters inked and painted on them are laid over the background painting and photographed. The artists who paint the backgrounds establish the mood and set the stage for the action. The combination of cel and painted background is called a "cel set-up" (catalogue numbers 16 and 77, for example). Because each cel represents characters in slightly different positions, many cels are photographed in succession on each background.

Long background paintings, like Greg Drolette's for *The Prince and the Pauper* (catalogue number 77), permit the illusion of camera movement, or panning, by moving the cel set-up beneath the stationary camera (the camera does not move).

Andy Warhol and Keith Haring
in Haring's studio

When photographed, each cel set-up represents 1/24th of a second of film time. (Sound films consist of 24 still frames per second, projected quickly enough to create an illusion of movement.) An eighty-minute animated feature film could require more than 1,200 cel set-ups and over 120,000 individual cels. No single artist could possibly execute all of these images.

Walt Disney ceased doing any of the actual drawing for his films in 1924, instead concentrating on the production and business aspects of his enterprise. Nothing in our exhibition was actually made by the hands of Walt Disney. (He was the voice of Mickey Mouse for twenty years, and would often say "There's a lot of the Mouse in me.")[7] But the procedure outlined above, and the look and feel of Disney films, were established by him and are used by the Walt Disney Company to this day. Disney died in 1966. We still speak of a "Disney" film even though Disney may not have done any of the actual drawing or even seen it.

Disney films are the ultimate in collaborative artworks, but the idea of many different artists creating a single work typifies popular (or commercial) art, from movies to posters, advertisements, product design, comics, magazines, billboards, and television programs.

When Andy Warhol said "That's probably one reason I'm using silkscreens now. I think somebody should be able to do all my paintings for me," he emulated the collaborative nature of Walt Disney's art and of popular art in general.[8] Like Disney, Warhol did not manually make all of his art, though in both cases the artist's judgment determined its every aspect. Warhol chose the images of his artworks and supervised their production when he did not actually make them.

Warren (1962) and *Troy* (1962–63) (catalogue numbers 79 and 80) are two of Warhol's earliest silkscreened images. After having painted the first set of *Campbell's Soup Cans* (1961–62) by hand,

Warhol discovered the photomechanical reproduction technique of photo silkscreen. For *Warren* and *Troy*, as with all of his early celebrity portraits, Warhol first chose an existing photograph that was made by someone else, then sent it to a lab with instructions to transfer it to a silkscreen. Then Warhol, or his assistants following his instructions, used the silkscreen to transfer the image to canvas or paper. When Warhol first did this in 1962, it was a departure from traditional fine art making for an artist not to make his art manually.[9] He imitated techniques that Disney had been using for decades.

While Warhol was obsessed with popular art, Keith Haring took a strong interest in the folk art of graffiti early in his career. Graffiti were greatly in evidence in New York in the early 1980s. In order to avoid arrest for vandalism, graffiti "writers" gave themselves nicknames, or "tags." L.A. II (Angel Ortiz) had several gallery shows with Haring in 1982–84 and collaborated with him on a number of works, among them *A Pair of Corinthian Columns* (catalogue number 120). Painted dayglo orange–an eye-catching color favored by graffiti artists–and drawn upon with ink by both artists, the columns resemble the architectural settings in which urban graffiti are usually seen.

If Haring both imitated the folk art of graffiti and collaborated with a graffiti writer in his early work, he also collaborated with image makers in the manner of popular art, like Disney and Warhol. Many of his images were made to be reproduced–in mass media, on consumer products like watches and T-shirts (catalogue number 195), on posters (catalogue number 181) and billboards (catalogue numbers 127, 154, and 176–77). Haring made the small (6³⁄₄ x 15 inches) drawing of a *Billboard Design for the Broward County Humane*

Society, Florida (catalogue number 154), then sent a photostat of it along with Pantone color chips to the billboard maker who enlarged the drawing, inserted the colors where Haring indicated them, and silkscreened the billboard in sections. The resulting 10″7′x 22″10′ *Billboard for the Broward County Humane Society, Florida* (catalogue number 155) was never actually touched by Haring. Although he also made a large body of unique, handmade artworks, this procedure typifies a whole category of Haring's objects.

Mass Media Haring intuitively understood that good mass-media imagery can be seen any size and still make a strong visual impact, like the *Drawing* and *Billboard for the Broward County Humane Society, Florida*. The absence of scale that typifies mass-media

imagery is atypical of fine art, yet it runs through most of Haring's art. His images can be enlarged or shrunk, like Disney's, which function as small drawings, as huge movie images, or in the scale of television.

Haring's bold, declarative style visually holds its own within a welter of other imagery. His individual images–like the barking dog, the Radiant Child (catalogue number 194), the strutting figure–are a kind of visual Esperanto that function like effective advertising and corporate logos. Haring's subway chalk drawings and other images began appearing in the world's mass media almost immediately after he made them. Reflecting the aggressiveness and quick take of mass-media imagery, they are eminently reproducible.

Using the most pervasive visual communication means of his time–mass media–Haring took his art out of galleries and museums, removed it from requiring the sanctions of art critics and collectors

before the public could see it, and presented it directly to his audience through the mass media. (For more about Haring and mass media, see the essay "The Radiant Child (Keith Haring)," pages 143–151.)

Their understanding of the mass media's visual dynamics is one of the many qualities Haring and Warhol share. The mass media when Warhol's fine art first emerged in the early 1960s were not the same as they were for Haring in the 1980s. The earliest evidence of television's pervasiveness and homogenizing effects occurred when the first generation raised on it came of age in the early 1960s. Color television first began to be widespread at about the same time. Another difference between the two artists is that Warhol was a commercial artist before becoming a fine artist, designing advertising from 1949 to 1960.

Warhol learned from advertising that the more times an image is repeated, the greater its impact. Repetition also expresses Warhol's fascination with the mass-media phenomenon of celebrity status, of being famous for being famous. Because the mass media create celebrities by repeating their images, they are unique to the mass-media era.

Warhol's repetition of images mimics advertising and mass-media celebrity making. The ten *Marilyn* prints (catalogue number 87) are in colors like early television sets with the color out of adjustment (as they often were), or out of skew as if the reception were bad (as it often was before cable). Repeating the images ten times suggests that they are all being received on different TV sets.

Warhol began a series of paintings and prints of Marilyn Monroe after she committed suicide on August 5, 1962. She was a perfect subject for him. Marilyn had been in the news during the Kennedy presidency for her sultry singing of "Happy Birthday" to the popular President at a huge party in Madison Square Garden. Also, her stormy marriages and her problematic career were the stuff of the tabloids. No doubt the allegations of Marilyn's affair with JFK (and/or his brother Bobby), and the supposed FBI confiscation of her telephone records following her death, contributed to Warhol's morbid interest in the dead actress. All of these aspects of her life were widely reported in the mass media, where Warhol obtained many of his subjects.

Warren and *Troy* (catalogue numbers 79 and 80) were made from Hollywood publicity stills silkscreened to look like television images with bad reception. *The Men in Her Life (Mike Todd and Eddie Fisher)* (catalogue number 78) was made from newspaper photographs depicting Liz Taylor's stormy love life that was trumpeted in the tabloids.

The images in *Jacqueline Kennedy* (catalogue number 83) came from newspaper and magazine photographs of the First Lady taken before and after her husband's assassination. The two images on the far right are details of the famous photograph taken aboard Air Force One before taking off from Dallas for Washington, D.C. Jackie was witnessing the swearing-in of Lyndon Johnson as President, replacing her dead husband whose body was also on the plane. The second image from the left is a reversed detail of a photo that appeared on the cover of *Life Magazine* on December 6, 1963. The full photograph depicts Mrs. Kennedy with her two children on the steps of the US Capitol watching JFK's casket descend the steps to begin the funeral cortege. Warhol cropped the photos to zoom in on the close-up, giving his paintings the "talking head" intimacy of television.

While Warhol and Haring used the mass media, Walt Disney created it. The entertainment monolith he masterminded includes movies, television, comics, books, theme parks, and all manner of consumer goods. Disney's genius for making imagery that was comprehensible to a huge international cross-section of people served as a role model to Haring and Warhol.

Not only Warhol and Haring, but the rest of the world admired Disney for brilliantly creating some of the best mass-media entertainment ever. Warhol and Haring aspired to have their images as widely known as Mickey Mouse and Donald Duck, which may be the most renowned images in the world. In the mass media, success is measured in the size of the audience reached. Disney's art may be the greatest mass-media art ever.

Mass Production   The traditional fine art idea of a one-of-a-kind image gives way in popular art to the idea of large numbers of identical, mass-produced images. Walt Disney's images have probably been more widely mass-produced than those of any other popular artist. Once the master negative for an animated film is made, hundreds of prints are manufactured, distributed, and shown simultaneously throughout the world. All the copies are equal in artistic status.

The one-of-a-kind Disney cels and drawings in our exhibition were not originally meant to be seen by the public. The Walt Disney Company discarded thousands of cels after the movies were made, considering them a means to an end rather than an end in themselves. Cels became highly prized only after the films began to be regarded as artworks in addition to entertainment.

The notion of mass production extends to Disney's most famous character, Mickey Mouse. Though Disney created the original character in 1928, many different artists have drawn Mickey since then. The *Steamboat Willie* drawings in our exhibition (catalogue num-

bers 1–5) were done by Ub Iwerks the same year as the first Mickey Mouse cartoons. In effect, Mickey Mouse himself was mass-produced, not only made into hundreds of identical prints of the same film but drawn by many different artists simultaneously. Yet, they are all more or less the same. In mass-production, uniqueness gives way to an aesthetic in which sameness is the most highly prized quality.

Warhol said "I like boring things. I like things to be exactly the same over and over again,"[10] and "I tried doing them by hand, but I find it easier to use a screen. This way, I don't have to work on my objects at all. One of my assistants or anyone else, for that matter, can reproduce the design as well as I could."[11]

Beginning in 1963, Warhol called his studio "The Factory" and employed assistants to make much of his art, like Walt Disney. For the *Marilyn* portfolio (catalogue number 87) 250 copies of each image were made by assistants on a production line. Workers contracted by the Los Angeles County Museum of Art made 100 of the *Kellogg's Boxes (Corn Flakes)* (catalogue number 91) following instructions Warhol sent from New York. (Warhol was having a show at LACMA and it was easier to make the boxes there than to ship them.) All of the copies of Warhol's mass-produced images are intentionally identical and of equal value and significance.

Like many popular artists (including Disney), Warhol used the camera as his primary means of mass production. Whether he appropriated a photograph from the mass media or made his own, transferring it to a photo silkscreen to make many identical images was the equivalent to using a photographic negative to make multiple copies of a photograph, similar to Disney printing many copies of his films from a master negative.

Yet Warhol made his silkscreened images on canvas, paper, and wood, the historically hallowed media of treasured fine art, not as disposable popular art forms like billboards and advertising posters. Warhol intentionally crossed over from fine art into popular art, blurring distinctions between the two but staying within the fine art traditions of painting and sculpture. Haring blurred the genres of visual imagery even further.

When Keith Haring opened the Pop Shop in 1986 with Warhol's encouragement, he established an equivalent to the Disney Company's licensed Disney Stores, where consumer goods featuring images from Walt Disney productions are sold. Haring's motivation was to make his images available at low cost to a populist audience. "I first went into the subways because I was cut out of the galleries. I've always been careful to be part of the popular culture. The Pop Shop is just keeping up with the original idea."[12]

T-shirts, buttons, and other mass-produced consumer goods bearing knock-offs of his images had begun turning up in Europe, Japan, Australia, South America, and Asia. "There were so many copies of my stuff around that I felt I had to do something myself so people would at least know what the real ones look like," Haring said.[13]

A retail outlet, the Pop Shop is like a gallery selling Haring's images in versions that are low cost because they are mass-produced but that equate with his more expensive art in the galleries, another retail outlet. As Haring said "We sold the inflatable baby and the toy radio and, mostly, a wide variety of T-shirts, because they're like a wearable print–they're art objects."[14]

Though Haring could have licensed some of his images and had them turn up on consumer products as often as Smurfs and Smiley Faces, he opened only two Pop Shops, in New York and Tokyo (the Tokyo Pop Shop is now closed). He wanted to maintain control over the presentation of his art to the public, and he felt that wider distribution would involve too many middle persons.

Regarding the Radiant Child image that Haring used so often, he said "People would love to buy the license, the people who manage the Garfield license and Peanuts. It would be huge money, I'm sure. Maybe that is a little hypocritical because I am saying I want it public and at the same time I want to keep it under my control. I still want to keep it art."[15]

Haring carried the distribution of fine art imagery further into the territory of popular art than any other fine artist before him, including Warhol. Generosity and genuine love for the people who like his art motivated him to make it affordable for anyone who wanted it. Taking his cue from popular art like Disney's, mass production became Haring's means to reach beyond the art world into the world at large.

Entertainers and Entertainment Beginning with his first artworks, Keith Haring often placed his art in the context of popular art and entertainment. His father entertained him at the kitchen table by drawing cartoons with his young son, fostering skills that made social points for him among his peers during childhood and youth. Except when he studied at the School of Visual Arts in New York City during 1978–79, Haring drew cartoons throughout his career.

For the catalogue of his first gallery show (at the Tony Shafrazi Gallery in 1982), Haring included a 32-page coloring book of cartoon-like images similar to those of his subway drawings. He intended it as a gift to children for their entertainment. For his birthday party in 1984, he installed an exhibition of his art, including *A Pair of Corinthian Columns* (catalogue number 120), at his favorite club, Paradise Garage. He called the celebration the *Party of Life I,* and invited 2,000 friends (about 3,000 showed up). Madonna, who had been a friend of Haring's since they were both fledgling artists on the lower East Side of Manhattan, sang *Like a Virgin* from her new album that had not yet been released.

In 1985 Haring painted a huge banner to be periodically unfurled on the dance floor of Steve Rubell's and Ian Schrager's popular club The Palladium. Artists Francesco Clemente, Kenny Scharf, and Jean-Michel Basquiat also painted and created environments in the Arata Isozaki-designed club. It is a sybaritic fantasy constructed within the shell of a crumbling theater on Fourteenth Street where rock 'n' roll concerts had been held. For a few years, the Palladium was the hippest night spot in New York.

Haring painted white, calligraphic designs on the bodies of the African American dancer and choreographer Bill T. Jones in 1983 and on the singer Grace Jones (not related to the choreographer) in 1985. Robert Mapplethorpe photographed Grace Jones, who asked Haring the following year to design a video for her song *I'm Not Perfect*. He painted a 60-foot-wide skirt that Jones rose up within as "all these people are following her and they go underneath the skirt, and the skirt consumes them as Grace floats away into the sky."[16]

Haring also designed several record album, cassette tape, and CD covers, among them a *Bipo Cover* (catalogue number 159) that includes the message "Crack is Wack," the subject of a large mural Haring painted alongside the freeway at 128th Street and Second Avenue in Manhattan.

The idea that his art be entertaining in the manner of popular culture affiliated Haring with popular entertainers like singers and placed his art in the context of clubs, CD and cassette covers, MTV videos, and other entertainments. Far from shunning them, Haring sought these outlets. He worked with the vernacular of popular culture and recognized that its

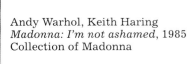

Andy Warhol, Keith Haring
Madonna: I'm not ashamed, 1985
Collection of Madonna

spaces were his spaces, that they were more likely to place his art before the eyes of the people he wanted to reach than art galleries and museums.

Andy Warhol first manifested his fascination with entertainers and entertainment when as a child he doted on Hollywood fan magazines and collected autographed photos of movie stars. He always wanted to be as famous as the celebrities he later painted. Warhol's most extravagant creation was his public persona, a fiction he created by controlling his image in the mass media. Using the mass media as one of his artistic media, Warhol made himself into a "part of American culture, like Mickey Mouse" according to Haring.[17]

Marilyn Monroe, Liz Taylor, Dolly Parton, Warren Beatty, Troy Donahue, Greta Garbo, James Dean, Ronald Reagan, the Marx Brothers, Grace Kelly, Mickey Mouse, Donald Duck, Dracula, Howdy Doody, and Superman are mass media celebrities and entertainers depicted by Warhol and represented in our exhibition (catalogue numbers 87, 78, 117–18, 79–80, 99, 113–14, 96, 111, 106, 115–16, 105, 104, and 101).

In 1966 Warhol *created* entertainment when he ran a discotheque for a month at the Dom in New York City, featuring light shows of his films projected on the walls. It was one of the earliest sound-and-light-show nightclubs. That same year, Warhol went on a concert tour with a rock band he helped to create, the *Velvet Underground* with Lou Reed and John Cale. Later he designed their first album cover featuring a banana-skin sticker that peeled off to reveal a flesh-colored banana underneath. Later still, he designed the Rolling Stones' *Sticky Fingers* album cover.

First Warhol depicted the stars, then he created them. When he made his film *Empire* in 1964, Warhol declared, "The Empire State Building is a star!"[18] Taking star-making another step, in 1969 he began publishing his own celebrity fan magazine, *Interview,* which became the contemporary mass-media equivalent to the movie star fan magazines of his youth.

From movie stars to his own movies and fan magazine, the shallow surface of America's entertainment was Warhol's subject matter. "If you want to know all about Andy Warhol," the artist said, "just look at the surface: of my paintings and films and me, and there I am. There's nothing behind it."[19] "I just pass my hands over the surface of things."[20]

Yet he knew that the surface is the soul of the mass media, where America lives imaginatively. That Warhol took the mundane events of American popular culture and made them the subject of his art gave the next generation, represented by Haring, the permission to go even further. "Whatever I've done would not have been possible without Andy," Haring said. "Had Andy not broken the concept of what art is supposed to be, I just wouldn't have been able to exist."[21]

Walt Disney's masterful entertainments are so widely known that nearly everyone on earth has seen at least one. His name is a household word. The Walt Disney Company created many firsts in entertainment history. The first fully synchronized sound cartoon, *Steamboat Willie* (catalogue numbers 1–5), in 1928, and the first feature-length animated cartoon, *Snow White and the Seven Dwarfs* (catalogue numbers 14–16 and 66), produced in the years 1934 to 1937, are but two examples.

Hundreds of millions of people have been entertained by the cartoon characters–the entertainers–Disney created. Between 1955 and 1985, 250 million people visited Disneyland. The number of people who have seen Disney films is incalculable. The Academy of Motion Picture Arts and Sciences recognized the quality of Disney films with 32 personal Academy Awards, while Disney and his company combined received 48 plus seven Emmys during Disney's lifetime. In terms of the number of people entertained and the quality of his entertainments, Disney may have been the greatest entertainer ever.

Greener Grass on the Other Side of the Fence
Though Disney enjoyed as high a status as any popular artist – maybe even the highest – he aspired to the presumably higher status of fine artist. *Fantasia,* a feature-length animated film including classical music and a cartoon ballet (catalogue numbers 53 – 60), was his bid for fine art status. It received good critical response but was not widely seen when first released because theaters where it was shown had to install expensive sound equipment. When motion picture theater sound technology caught up with Disney, the film became a widely seen classic. For Disney, the initial frustration in attempting to cross over into fine art must have felt similar to the first response from the fine art establishment that greeted Warhol's and Haring's incursions into popular art.

To all three artists, the grass was greener on the other side of the fence. Disney started out as a popular artist, achieved the highest standing, and attempted to reach the status of fine artist. Warhol started as a commercial artist, made the transition into being a fine artist, yet always aspired to have his art as widely accepted as that of the best popular artists, like Disney. Haring benefited from the dual accomplishments of Disney and Warhol, aspiring to situate his art somewhere in between the two. Partly because his career lasted only a short ten years compared with Warhol's four decades (if you count Warhol's thirteen-year commercial art career, too), Haring never gained universal acclaim within the fine art establishment.

I suspect that one of the reasons why some guardians of fine art resist admitting Haring into the pantheon that includes Andy Warhol is related to why Walt Disney was not taken seriously by the intelligentsia: their art appeals to children and young people. It is, consequently, not regarded as "serious." Warhol's art, however much it appeals to youth because of its mass-media content, has a cynical undercurrent. When his art does not deal with death, disaster, and tragedy – from car crashes to electric chairs to race riots, plane crashes, and assassinations – it often depicts the transitory nature of celebrity status. Warhol's art is mostly about a sense of loss: loss of life, loss of innocence, potential loss of status. Haring's and Disney's art, equally steeped in popular culture, are more optimistic and affirmative. The animated lines in their drawings contain a gregarious energy that conveys the optimism of youth. They jump off the page with movement. Warhol's lines, as beautiful as they are, just lie there.

Haring and Disney sought to create a universal visual language that was attuned to popular culture, especially to the popular culture of youth. Popular culture is a primary link they both share with Warhol. Like a tripod, Haring kept one foot in the fine art camp, one in popular art, and a third in the folk art camp of graffiti. He crossed over into and blurred the distinctions between the three primary categories of visual imagery, with the result that the critical criteria of none – but all – apply to his art. For Haring, the grass was greenest on every side of the fence.

The exhibition at the Phoenix Art Museum

Disney in Context

by Bruce Hamilton
with text about Carl Barks by Geoffrey Blum

Matching Cels to Backgrounds   In the late 1930s, Walt Disney entered into an agreement with the Courvoisier Galleries of San Francisco to sell original art from Disney's animated films–both the cartoon shorts and the newly completed feature *Snow White and the Seven Dwarfs*. In the process, decisions had to be made on what to sell and how to present it to the public. Much of the art that is still extant does not survive in the same form or context as it enjoys on the screen; seldom can we match a piece of Disney art to the finished frame from its film. Reconstructing those marketing decisions helps us to understand why.

Each frame of finished film begins with a background painting. Since the animator's camera is fixed in place, the background itself must be moved to give the impression that our eyes are sweeping across a panorama. In the early days, such "pan" backgrounds were generally watercolors a foot high and several feet in length. Depending on the illusion required, some were even painted in a blur to suggest rapid motion.

Next come one or more layers of transparent celluloid and, as the top slice of the sandwich, perhaps a bit of foreground art. The cartoon characters or special effects that we see in motion on screen are inked onto these cels and painted in color on the reverse. Gouache pigments opaque the figures, so that they appear to have been painted onto the background when the cels are laid down to be photographed. Twenty-four such cels are made for every second of film, each frame showing only a tiny change in the position of the figures. Once a cel has been photographed, it is removed from the background, and the next in sequence is put in its place. When these still photographs are projected in rapid succession on the screen, the figures come to life. This often involves placing hundreds of cels against one master background.

Here was the first problem for Disney and Courvoisier: background art was limited. While some rejected backgrounds could be used and even a few pans could be chopped up, there would never be enough to pair with the thousands of celluloids for sale. The only thing to do was to create new backgrounds, some of which could be called no more than backings. Perhaps a quick job of airbrushing was done, or a character in full figure might be placed against a field of wood veneer–whatever looked good. Because the cels sold for very little, not much time was put into these substitute backgrounds. Rarely did they simulate what appeared on the screen.

Disney also believed that the cels, painted on heavy-gauge nitrate-cellulose, trademarked Celluloid, would dull the beauty and brightness of the backgrounds. Worse, after all the undesirable cels were culled, the remaining ones might not fit right over the available backgrounds. Both problems were solved by trimming out the characters and gluing them directly into the background art, positioning them wherever they looked best. The idea was that each set-up (that is, a cel with background) should be sold as a unit suitable for framing and must therefore have the greatest possible customer appeal.

There were no collectors then, not as we know them today; only "savers" who kept their cels and set-ups for the simple joy the images gave them. The people who bought them from Courvoisier devoted little thought to the authenticity of their pictures. What *was* authentic, anyway? There were no rules concerning the marketing of animation art in the 1930s. Besides, every piece at the Courvoisier Galleries came from Disney with a certificate of authenticity!

25

There were other hurdles to overcome in preparing the cel set-ups. Characters' shadows were animated on separate cels. These would have been difficult to cut out and glue together with the figures in the Courvoisier art, so shadows were routinely airbrushed onto the watercolor backgrounds. Today this practice would raise numerous eyebrows, but customers back then often considered the whole process of animation unfathomable and rarely questioned what they saw. Those few buyers who did understand the basics of animation must have wondered how the shadow of a moving figure could be permanently fixed to a stationary setting. It is also troubling today for the purist to see cels from certain films mounted on backgrounds from other films. *Brave Little Tailor* is a case in point (catalogue number 29). The cel of Mickey Mouse is clearly from the 1938 short that bears its name, but the watercolor background comes from a Silly Symphony called *Music Land* produced three years earlier. Visually it is not a bad match; only when you look closely at the art can you see that Mickey is seated on a flat surface and not on the curb against which he has been placed. Numerous cels from *Brave Little Tailor*, including several others in this exhibition, were packaged by Courvoisier with what only appears to be appropriate backgrounds. The art may have been jumbled at the Disney Studio; or perhaps no thought was given to the pairing. If it looked good, what did it matter?

"Ferdinand and Matador" from *Ferdinand the Bull* (catalogue number 35) shows a different kind of backdrop used extensively with the Disney cels, a simple wood veneer. Then there is the frame-and-patterns design accompanying the close-up of "Snow White (with Rabbits)" from *Snow White and the Seven Dwarfs* (catalogue number 14)–another type of background produced in quantity for Courvoisier. And the two figures in *Donald's Penguin* (catalogue number 52) are set against one of many identical airbrushed backdrops that were made to display trimmed figures of Donald and his pet Tootsie. Strictly speaking, none of these backgrounds is authentic, but all are typical of Courvoisier's marketing methods and are accepted today as such.

In contrast to the Courvoisier cel set-ups, the exhibition includes "Snow White (with the Prince in the Forest)" from *Snow White and the Seven Dwarfs* (catalogue number 16), a stunning cel set-up of Snow White and her prince on horseback, beautifully matched to a master background from the film and even complete with the appropriate foreground art.

Problems of Preservation Such examples are rare. Walt Disney himself considered the cels of little permanent value; after all, they were merely ink-and-color tracings from pencil sketches produced by higher-paid artists. If they could be washed clean at the conclusion of a film and re-used, well and good; otherwise they were routinely discarded. Animator Ward Kimball gleefully tells the story of tying bunches of cels to the soles of his shoes and skating down the studio corridors on them.

Background paintings, on the other hand, were more likely to be treasured as works of art. Despite the volume of cels used in making one of those early shorts, a greater percentage of original backgrounds survives today. This was not entirely a matter of choice. As the years passed, the sheets of old nitrate frequently disintegrated, depending on how they were stored. Highly flammable, some crumbled into foul-smelling dust. With the risk of spontaneous combustion, many were prudently discarded as a fire hazard. The risk seemed to compound according to volume, when many cels were stacked tightly in an airless container. Modern collectors will be happy to hear that the trimmed and framed cels which have survived the last half-century are relatively safe.

Old nitrates also turn green, get cloudy, and wrinkle. Restorers can often clean and polish these artworks, bringing back much of their original luster, but the process requires washing off the old paint and applying a new coat, a practice that purists find objectionable. So the clock on these ancient cels continues to tick.

Recently, the Walt Disney Company has learned the value – commercial as well as aesthetic – of keeping key backgrounds from each of its cartoons, matched with top-flight cels from the appropriate scenes. That is how it was possible for Disney to provide this exhibition with a cel set-up from *The Prince and the Pauper* (catalogue number 77). It is instructive to study this artwork, a pan background with untrimmed cels (note the overlapping edges). Had this art been sold by Courvoisier, the figures would have been cut out of the cel sheets and the ends of the background lopped off. Note also that today's cels are made of a clearer, more durable material that will not age like the old nitrate, though they still dim the clarity of a background, especially in multiple cell set-ups. Collectors and curators are divided on the solution to this problem. At a recent auction of artworks from *Who Framed Roger Rabbit?*, most of the cels were cut out; a subsequent offering of material from *The Little Mermaid* was left untrimmed. Both sales were criticized – one for trimming, the other for not doing so. But everyone admits the rarity and the historical value of the Courvoisier material, trimmed or untrimmed.

Ub Iwerks and the Birth of Mickey Collectors and scholars also agree on the pivotal importance of Mickey Mouse in the development of Disney's art, reflected here not only in the celluloids but in a selection of the pencil drawings from which they were traced. Disney could be extravagant at times, but he did not believe in waste; he insisted that these animation drawings, the essence of all motion in his cartoons, be kept for possible future use. Thanks to the filing system of the studio's animation research library, it has been possible to locate original drawings to match some of the key cels in the exhibition. For instance, the cel set-up depicting the famous fly-swatting scene from *Brave Little Tailor* (catalogue number 17) is paired with a sequence of animation drawings by Les Clark (catalogue numbers 18–26). But we are getting ahead of our story.

When Walt Disney moved from Kansas City to set up his own film studio on the west coast, he brought with him a young animator named Ub Iwerks. It was Iwerks who gave Mickey his early look and who almost single-handedly animated the early Mickey Mouse cartoons. The mouse was first animated in 1928 in a silent short called *Plane Crazy*. Because Walt Disney was unable to sell the silent film, Disney delayed its release and preceded it with *Steamboat Willie*, the first Mickey Mouse short to be seen by the public and the first cartoon to feature a fully synchronized soundtrack. Iwerks, an exceptionally fast artist, turned out hundreds of Mickey drawings on a daily basis, including the five shown here from *Steamboat Willie* (catalogue numbers 1–5). The movement as represented in this sequence has several in-between drawings omitted from the grouping better to showcase the rotation of the mouse's figure.

27

To study Iwerks' pencil drawings is to realize the effortlessness of his art: the lack of preliminary sketch lines, the bold and simple strokes, and the rubber-limbed quality he imparted to Mickey, which gave the mouse such freedom of movement. Mickey's head and lower body are each rendered in one quick circle, as are the buttons on his trademark short pants. The only concession to a finished look comes in the partial circles Iwerks drew for Mickey's ears, a clever, two-dimensional concept that keeps the ears in perpetual round silhouette whatever the angle we view them from. The inkers who placed blank cels over these pencil drawings to trace the line art had an easy job, and doubtless it became easier with each cartoon because of Iwerks' incredible consistency.

In those early black and white cartoons, however, the artists were still feeling their way. Disney realized that having just one animator on a cartoon–even a speed demon like Iwerks–was limiting. Forcing several men to draw in precisely the same style was not practical. So Walt instructed his best artists to prepare model sheets, guide drawings to establish the look of each cartoon. That still was not enough to guarantee consistency because some artists are simply better than others. Disney's solution, obviously following the lead of earlier studios, was to have his best animators draw only the "extremes," the biggest takes and the major changes in a figure's movement and expression. With a hyperactive character like Donald Duck, these sketches might fall in direct sequence, but more often they would skip two or more intermediate drawings. Less experienced artists were assigned to prepare "in-betweens" using the extremes as guidelines.

In later years, when a large number of animators would all work on one project, even less was left to chance. There would be rough animation drawings and clean-up animation drawings, the latter polishing discrepancies which had been left for the inkers to catch in the 1920s. Examples of this highly refined team animation can be seen in rough animation drawings by Andreas Deja and the clean-up animation drawings by Kathy Bailey, both for *The Prince and the Pauper* (catalogue numbers 69–76). Other drawings of note are the extremes prepared by Ward Kimball, one of the studio's legendary Nine Old Men, to animate a scene from *Ferdinand the Bull* (catalogue numbers 36–41), and Howard Swift's delicate pencil drawings for the "Dance of the Hours" segment from *Fantasia* (catalogue numbers 54–59).

Ferdinand Horvath, Talent behind the Scenes   As the Disney cartoons became famous, requests poured in from all over the world for an original drawing, always presumed to be from the hand of Walt Disney who, many people thought, drew everything himself. It may have been partly to answer this demand that the studio entered into its agreement with Courvoisier; but before that happened, many anomalous bits of art were distributed in a more haphazard fashion, and today these curiosities pose a problem in varying degrees for the unwary collector. *Mickey with a Lasso* (catalogue number 64) is certainly a pencil sketch of Mickey but not an animation drawing, and though it is signed "Walt Disney," the sketch is clearly not Walt's. On occasion, one or another staff artist would do a sketch that Disney would sign and give away, but as his workload increased more and more often he had the artists ape his signature as a matter of routine. After his rise to fame, Walt rarely had the time to draw Mickey; and faced with many superior talents on his staff, perhaps he also lacked the inclination. Aside from a few rough sketches on menu covers, or impromptu doodles on whatever bit of paper was handy, Disney did not make drawings of Mickey for his adoring public.

And still the studio was besieged with requests. So a series of presentation ink drawings was made and printed in black on high-quality paper that would take watercolor. *Minnie and Mickey at a Piano*, taken from the 1932 *Mickey Mouse* cartoon "The Wayward Canary" (catalogue number 65) is one of these hand-colored prints inscribed by a staff artist. This was a common practice, used generally by newspaper cartoonists who received more requests for drawings than they could accommodate. Mrs. Elly Horvath, widow of the artist Ferdinand Huszti Horvath, has claimed that her husband drew the pictures reproduced in these prints. Research in the Disney archives has failed to prove or disprove this claim.

Horvath himself remains an enigma. Unlike much of the Disney talent, he was an accomplished artist with an established European reputation well before he came to the studio. Disney hired him to provide ideas and concept paintings that could kick-start a cartoon and inspire the other artists. This Horvath did, churning out thousands of idea sketches, mostly in color and almost always signed – something the rest of the staff rarely did.[1] Since artists at the studio were expected to wear several hats, he also painted backgrounds for the early color shorts – some of the most beautiful watercolors to emerge from the studio at this period. The rest of the time he kept to himself and remained a talent behind the scenes.

Disney's respect for Horvath can be seen in the way he made use of the artist's concepts, notably the pencil inspiration of the evil forest in *Snow White and the Seven Dwarfs* (catalogue number 8). One of a dozen similar sketches that surfaced years ago in the Horvath estate, it shows a tangle of dark, gnarled trees reaching clawlike limbs to snatch at the fleeing Snow White. The final backgrounds and animation in the film are remarkably close to Horvath's drawing in detail and spirit.

During his tenure at the studio in the 1930s, Horvath worked on possibly forty animated films, most of them Silly Symphonies. He is not known to have made animation drawings or to have participated in the assembly-line aspects of cartooning, yet his artwork shines through, occasionally in surprising places. The one-sheet poster titled *Silly Symphonies "The Practical Pig"* (catalogue number 45), showing a wacky scene in which the Big Bad Wolf disguises himself as a mermaid, is based on one of his sketches. It is an improbable gag and an unlikely choice for a poster, yet there it is, a virtual duplicate of a color concept drawn by Horvath. If we accept his widow's contention that Horvath drew the presentation pieces described earlier, could he not have made the original art for the one-sheet as well? Since the poster art is unsigned and studio records from the 1930s are sketchy at best, we can only speculate; but the inking style is reminiscent of other works by Horvath.

Posters and Promotional Art This leads us to another facet of Disney animation art and another type of relic, the vintage cartoon poster. Because of limited production and distribution, these posters are in scarce supply today; the ones generally regarded as common may survive in no more than fifty copies. Two of the posters in this exhibition are not even preserved in the Disney archives and are believed to be one of a kind: the ones for *Silly Symphonies "Little Hiawatha"* and *Mickey Mouse "Magician Mickey"* (catalogue numbers 11–12). Called "forty by sixties" because of their unusual dimensions, these silkscreen prints are two of only a handful of this type of Disney poster that are known to have survived from the 1930s. Each is thought to have been made for the premiere of its respective cartoon. The artists who drew them are unknown.

The exhibition's one-sheet[2] from *Mickey Mouse – "The Mad Doctor"* (catalogue number 6) is historic for another reason. This dark, almost wicked image reflects the popularity of horror films in the 1930s and shows how Disney's artists would often borrow a subject or a mood from mainstream cinema. Though the black and white Mickey Mouse film was neither as spooky nor as colorful as its poster, it inspired comic strip artist Floyd Gottfredson to draw one of his best newspaper serials, "Blaggard Castle," a frightening tale of Mickey and his friends in the clutches of three mad scientists. Comics historian Thomas Andrae, who interviewed Gottfredson extensively, reports that the artist "augmented the Gothic atmosphere of his strip by modeling his scientists on Boris Karloff from a movie he had just seen. He gave them the dark, deep-set eyes of the homicidal butler played by Karloff in *The Old Dark House* (1932)."[3] So there was constant artistic crossover between the different popular media. What was current in the movies could influence Disney's animated shorts; these in turn might be spun off into newspaper strips, children's books, and magazine features.

Among the various publicity materials the Disney studio would circulate to promote each new cartoon was a set of eight photographs, most of them prints of key frames, or "stills," from the film. Because this halftone art did not print well in newspapers, the studio would also mix in two or three line drawings made specifically for reproduction. Drawn in advance of the film's release, these would constitute the first illustrations made from Disney's new cartoon – a major point for collectors and historians.

Silly Symphonies "The Wise Little Hen" (catalogue number 7) is a publicity drawing of the hen, Peter Pig, and Donald Duck. Though the first two characters are largely forgotten today, and the drawing could not possibly have been thought of as historic in 1934, it is now generally regarded as the first illustration of Donald Duck. Only production art – concepts, story sketches, animation drawings, and cels – would have preceded it.

The year 1934 was a banner one for Disney. Donald's birth proved to be the second greatest event in the studio's history, for the duck grew rapidly in popularity. On his first appearance he played a small supporting role, but that was enough for him to steal the show from the Wise Little Hen – and eventually from Mickey Mouse. At first sight, the early Donald was nothing more than a duck in a sailor suit, and one prone to terrible tantrums and bouts of incoherent quacking. Yet it soon became clear that he was the perfect antithesis to noble little Mickey, and a far better vehicle for comedy. Donald was Everyman, a struggling, complaining, charming failure of a character with whom children and adults alike could identify. Over the next two years, the studio paired him with Mickey in most of the mouse's cartoons, giving Donald increasingly meaty roles, until at last in 1937 he starred in his own short, *Don Donald*. The rest is history; some of Disney's greatest artists would build their careers working with the duck.

Carl Barks and the Duck Phenomenon Indeed, no discussion of Disney's magical drawings would be complete without a nod in the direction of Carl Barks, who has done more than any other artist to shape the look and personality of Donald Duck. In part this achievement is due to the length of Barks' tenure with Donald. He began drawing the duck in 1935 and now, at the age of ninety-one, continues to work on lithographs and sculptures featuring his feathered creation. Perhaps it was his stamina that Disney had in mind when the company honored him recently as one of the Disney Legends. No other artist in the history of the studio has labored so long or so faithfully on a single character.

Unlike many of his colleagues, Barks was a late bloomer. He signed with Disney at the age of thirty-four, his only qualification being a seven-year stint as cartoonist on the *Calgary Eye-Opener,* a mildly risqué girlie magazine published in Minneapolis. Today his sketches of leggy nudes, dour matrons, and suffering husbands seem sexist, but in the 1930s they tapped a major vein of folk humor and gave Barks the sense of working within a tradition. His gaffers and flappers owe a little to Howard Chandler Christy, something more to James Montgomery Flagg, and much to the Sunday comics the artist had loved as a boy. All this would stand him in good stead when he went to work for Walt Disney, whose animated films relied heavily on deft characterization and broad jokes involving battles of the sexes.

Barks started as an in-betweener but Walt quickly found that the artist's talent was for narrative rather than motion. In an attempt to break away from the exacting and tedious end of animation, Barks began submitting plot ideas for Mickey Mouse cartoons. One of his jokes pitting Donald Duck against a mechanical barber chair so impressed Disney that the producer paid an extra fifty dollars for the gag, completed the cartoon as a duck short, and transferred Barks to the story department. The artist was beginning to make his presence felt.

This was to be Barks' journeyman period – again a stretch of seven years. Teamed at first with veteran storymen, he learned how to create new characters and became instrumental in the birth of Daisy Duck, Donald's nephews, and Gus Goose. Daisy, being little more than a stereotype, enjoyed relatively few innings on the screen, but Barks soon realized that the nephews had potential and pro-

ceeded to flesh out their personalities. Gus, in contrast, had a long and difficult birth and was featured at last in only one cartoon, *Donald's Cousin Gus* (catalogue numbers 50–51 represent the poster and a drawing of it).[4] If we look through the massive files of sketches extant at the Disney archives, we can see that it was Barks' gags about the goose's appetite which finally crystallized the character, gave Gus his charm, and provided a theme to tie the cartoon together. In addition, the artist was instrumental in giving the goose his rounded look and the long, supple neck that we see on the film's one-sheet (catalogue number 51).

At this time Barks was also developing story formulas that would propel his writing in later years: jokes about troublesome pets and wayward mechanical devices based on his early life as a rural laborer. Again we see the individual vision coloring the final Disney product, with *Donald's Penguin* being a case in point. Most of the gags in the finished cartoon and even the art for the final cel set-ups (catalogue number 52) can be traced back to storyboard drawings by Barks.

Since Disney animation is a group effort, it cannot be said that Barks ever controlled the screen portrayal of Donald; but as

his sketches grew in charm and refinement, the animators came to rely on them, following his layout, staging, and facial expressions in preparing the finished films. Had he remained at the studio, Barks might have become a director. Instead he chose to break away in 1942 and pursue a new career drawing the duck for a fledgling line of comic books. His achievements in this realm over the next 25 years were prodigious. Working out of his house, Barks both wrote and drew nearly 500 stories, reshaping Donald's personality and expanding the range of his mind and activities. To the Disney studio, these comics were never more than a merchandising spin-off; but to millions of loyal readers around the world, they constituted *the* portrayal of Donald Duck.

As it turned out, the comics carried Barks into further artistic endeavors well past his official retirement in 1966. While he was heaving a sigh of relief and settling into a rocking chair, his readers–now grown to adulthood–sought him out. When they heard that he had begun to dabble in oil paints, they set up a clamor for pictures of the ducks. In an unusually generous move, the Disney studio granted permission for Barks to make paintings of its characters; and by the time that permission was withdrawn in 1976, the artist had produced 122 oil paintings on subjects from his comic books.

Here is where the Disney ducks take on dimensions so new as to create problems for the scholar and the curator. What are these paintings–kitsch? fine art? Reportedly, one fan asked for a picture of the ducks together with Jesus Christ; Barks resoundingly vetoed the idea. Having worked more than 50 years in the Disney vein of realism, something that animators Frank Thomas and Ollie Johnston call "the illusion of life,"[5] Barks remains a staunch traditionalist. He has always claimed that the ducks were a species of human being "meet[ing] their problems with the everyday weapons that we have to use in our own lives."[6] When he undertook to paint the characters in 1971, he tried to visualize them in three dimensions, studying the effects of light on round shapes and placing them in wholly natural settings researched in the same sourcebook that had fueled his comics for 25 years: the *National Geographic Magazine*. His oil paintings are solidly representational.

Halloween in Duckburg (catalogue number 67), painted in 1973, illustrates this aspect of Barks' art. At first glance, the picture is a fantasy of fanged demons and pink hobgoblins that make talking ducks seem sedate by comparison. Yet the lighting is natural, the perspective exact, and every mischievous detail of monsters is anatomically credible. We are also inclined to accept the fantasy because of long-standing folkloric traditions about Halloween. Barks knew all this, and knew just how far he could stretch our credulity and still maintain the illusion of life. He based the painting on a comic book he had drawn in 1952 (*Donald Duck* 26)–specifically on his cover design, which featured Donald, Witch Hazel, and the nephews at the door, but no monsters. These constitute a later addition, expanding the vertical image to a horizontal format and giving the artist's imagination greater room to flex itself. The book in turn was based on a Disney short called *Trick or Treat,* and while Barks had no hand in scripting the film, he noodled with the story while adapting it to comic book format. Finally, it is not too hard to see in Witch Hazel shadows of the grumpy old harridans that populated Barks' *Calgary Eye-Opener* cartoons. So the picture, like the harvest moon that lights it, brings us full circle, encapsulating Barks' career.

Gustaf Tenggren, Old World Master   It is always Walt Disney's name that appears on the films, posters, books, comics, toys–and of course the copyright notices. Yet without the help of extraordinary artists like Iwerks, Horvath, Barks, and the Nine Old Men, there would be no Disney mythos. This catalogue can note only a few of the brightest talents; there were many others. At the same time, due credit must be given to Disney himself. At one time or another, all his artists have acknowledged that it was Walt's guidance, his insight and his vision, that orchestrated their diverse talents into one master symphony.

Pinocchio, perhaps the greatest of the studio's animated features, stands as a lasting tribute to this vision. Combining as it does the talents of countless artists, background painters, and animators, the film is a major feat of teamwork; and today, more than 50 years after its premiere, it remains unchallenged for innovation, technical expertise, and visual beauty. Once again, some of the overall glamor can be traced back to the work of one man: Swedish artist Gustaf Tenggren, who painted the richly hued watercolor concepts for *Snow White* and whom Disney commissioned to do the same for *Pinocchio.* As Christopher Finch has observed, Tenggren's delicate studies in line and wash contributed greatly to the look of both films, toning down their color schemes and giving them an aged, old-world quality.[7] The *Pinocchio* and *Snow White* Courvoisier cel set-ups in this exhibition can only hint at the beauty of the finished films (catalogue numbers 63 and 14–15).

So the final highlight of our exhibition is Tenggren's concept for the opening scene of *Pinocchio* (catalogue number 13), a street full of children running home from school to see the wooden puppet in the window of Geppetto's workshop. This picture is a masterpiece of authentic detail. Tenggren knew the people he was portraying, the way they lived, how they built their towns–how they dealt, for instance, with problems of rain and waste water. He painted windows with streaks just below their corners, stains deposited over the years by rivulets of rusty rain or splashed from panfuls of dishwater discarded into the street. He pictured rooftop gutters snaking around the sides of buildings so that they would empty into some dim back courtyard and not the public thoroughfare. And he made his narrow, uneven, and cobbled street with one center gutter to keep floodwater from spilling over into the basements of the ancient shops and houses. It is amazing to think that this painting was never intended for publication or display. All that for a cartoon!

We have taken only the briefest of peeks behind the scenes. The great work of animation goes on, and legends surrounding Walt Disney and his studio continue to proliferate. There have been many shows of Disney art before, sometimes combined with other studios, but there has never been an exhibition quite like this one. The current exhibition reveals how deeply Walt Disney's art has become ingrained in American culture by demonstrating its impact on two generations of contemporary American fine artists.

1–5 *Steamboat Willie*, animation drawings, set of 5, 1928

7 *Silly Symphonies "The Wise Little Hen,"* 1934

8 "Snow White in the Evil Forest" from
Snow White and the Seven Dwarfs, c. 1936

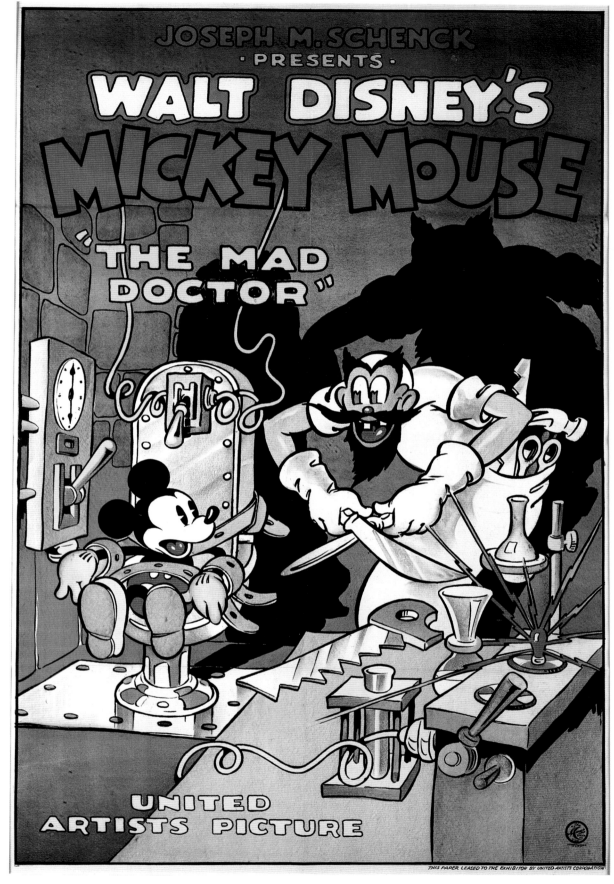

6   *Mickey Mouse, "The Mad Doctor," 1933*

9 *Little Hiawatha*, Courvoisier cel set-up, 1937

10   *Little Hiawatha (with his pants down)*, Courvoisier cel set-up, 1937

11   *Silly Symphonies "Little Hiawatha," 1937*

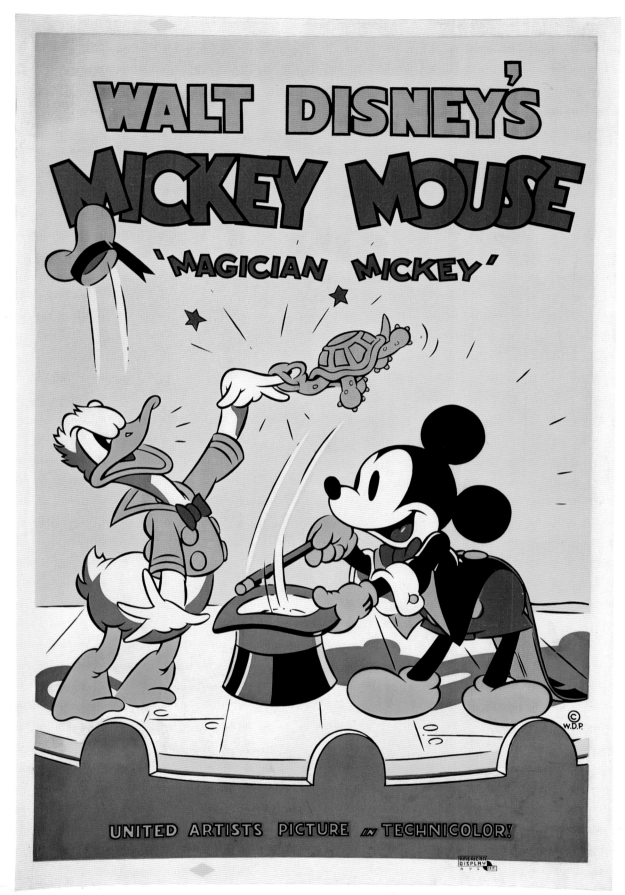

12 *Mickey Mouse "Magician Mickey," 1937*

13   *Pinocchio* (original concept of the opening scene), c. 1937

14 "Snow White (with Rabbits)" from
Snow White and the Seven Dwarfs, Courvoisier cel set-up, 1937

15   "Snow White (at a window)" from
Snow White and the Seven Dwarfs, Courvoisier cel set-up, 1937

16   "Snow White (with the Prince in the Forest)" from
Snow White and the Seven Dwarfs, cel set-up, 1937

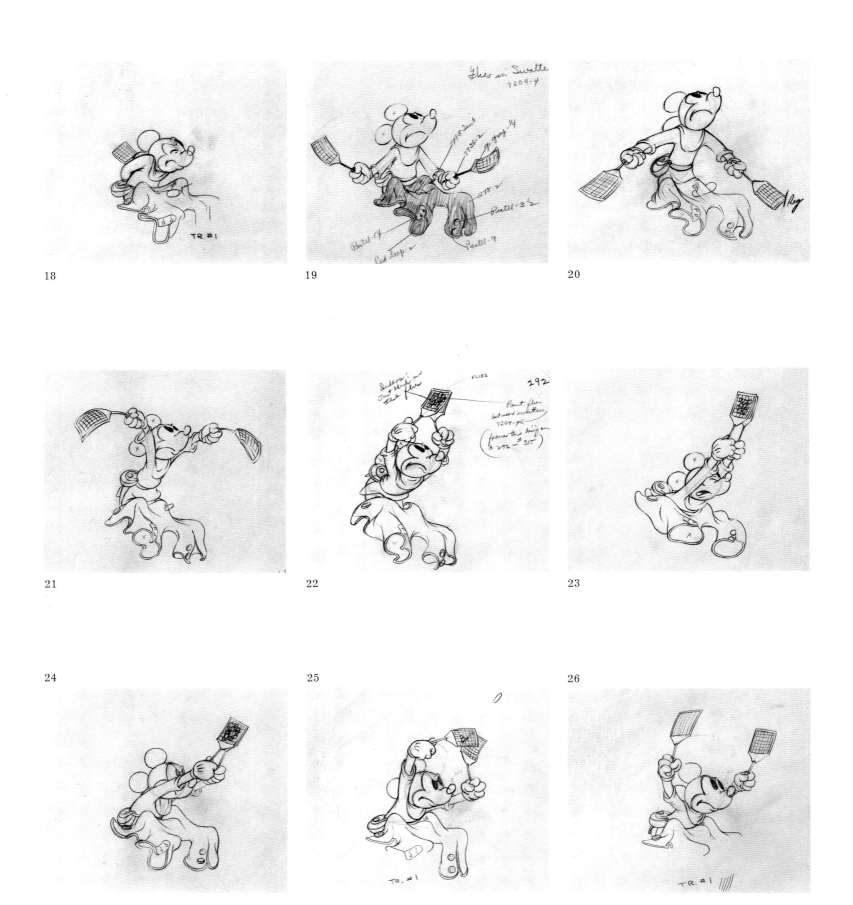

18

19

20

21

22

23

24

25

26

18–26   *Brave Little Tailor*, clean-up animation extremes, set of 9, 1938

17   *Brave Little Tailor*, Courvoisier cel set-up, 1938

27   *Brave Little Tailor*, cel set-up, 1938

28 *Brave Little Tailor*, cel set-up, 1938

29   *Brave Little Tailor*, cel set-up, 1938

30   *Brave Little Tailor*, cel set-up, 1938

31 *Brave Little Tailor*, cel set-up, 1938

32　*Brave Little Tailor*, cel set-up, 1938

33   *Brave Little Tailor*, cel set-up, 1938

34 *Society Dog Show*, cel set-up, 1938

36

37

38

39

40

41

36–41   *Ferdinand the Bull*, clean-up animation extremes, set of 6, 1938

35 "Ferdinand and Matador" from
Ferdinand the Bull, Courvoisier cel set-up, 1938

42   *The Pointer*, cel set-up, 1939

44   *The Pointer*, cel set-up, 1939

43   *The Pointer*, 1939

45   *Silly Symphonies "The Practical Pig,"* 1939

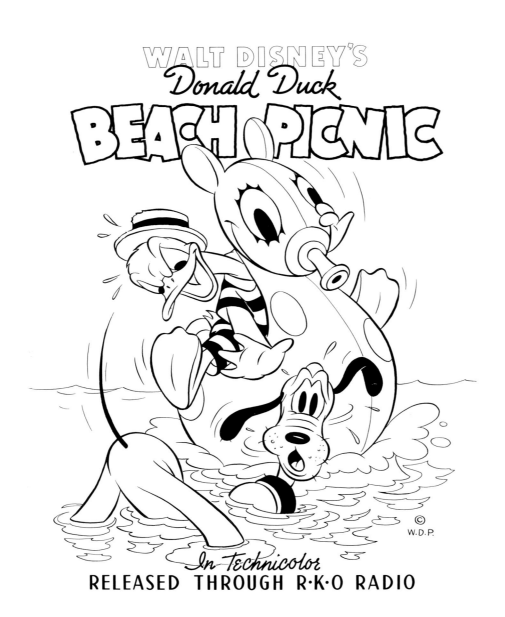

Donald Duck "Beach Picnic," 1939

47 *Donald Duck "Beach Picnic," 1939*

48   *The Ugly Duckling*, Courvoisier cel set-up, 1939

49　*The Practical Pig*, Courvoisier cel set-up, 1939

50   *Donald's Cousin Gus*, 1939

51   *Donald's Cousin Gus, 1939*

52 *Donald's Penguin, "Donald Duck and Tootsie," Courvoisier cel set-up, 1939*

53 *Fantasia,* cel set-up, 1940

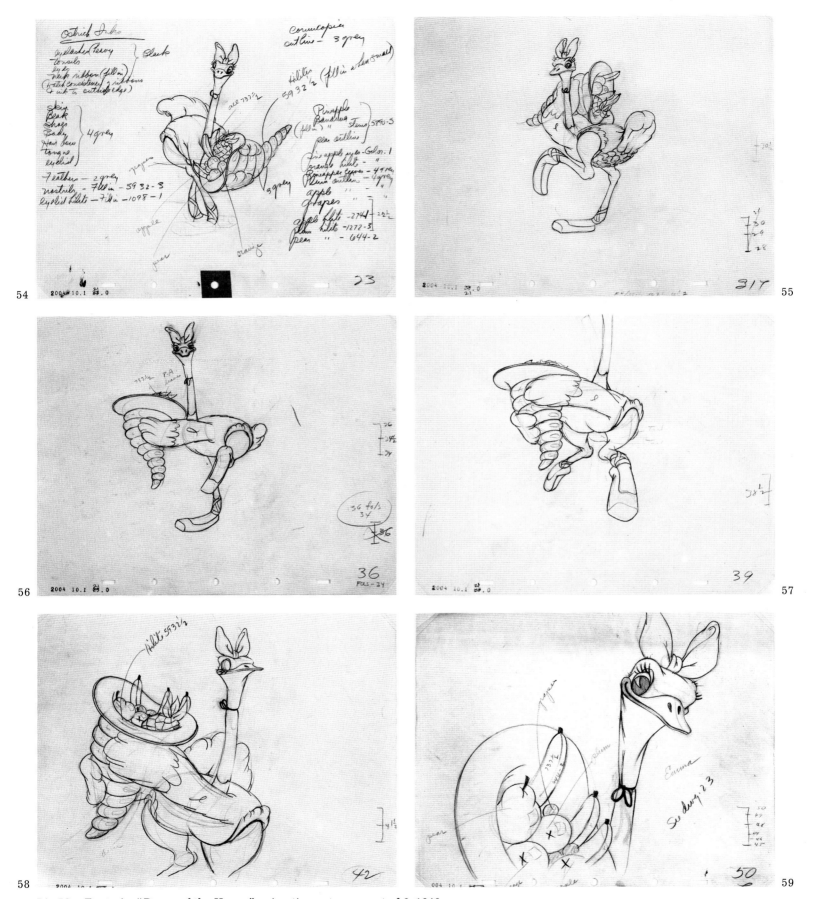

54–59 *Fantasia,* "*Dance of the Hours,*" animation extremes, set of 6, 1940

60   *Fantasia, "Dance of the Hours,"* Courvoisier cel set-up, 1940

61   *Jiminey*, from "*Pinocchio*," Courvoisier cel set-up, 1940

62 *Jiminey*, from "*Pinocchio*," Courvoisier cel set-up, 1940

63   *Cleo*, from "*Pinocchio*," Courvoisier cel set-up, 1940

64   *Mickey with a Lasso*, not dated

65   *Minnie and Mickey Mouse at Piano*, not dated

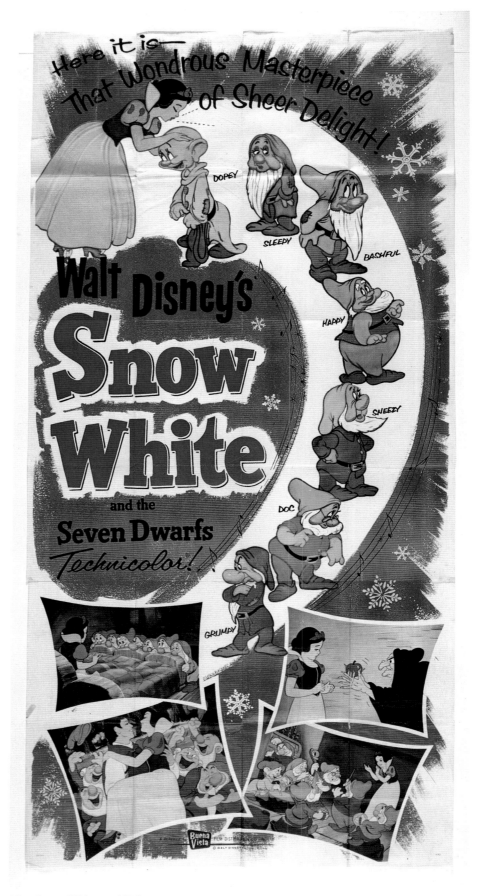

66   *Snow White, c. 1953*

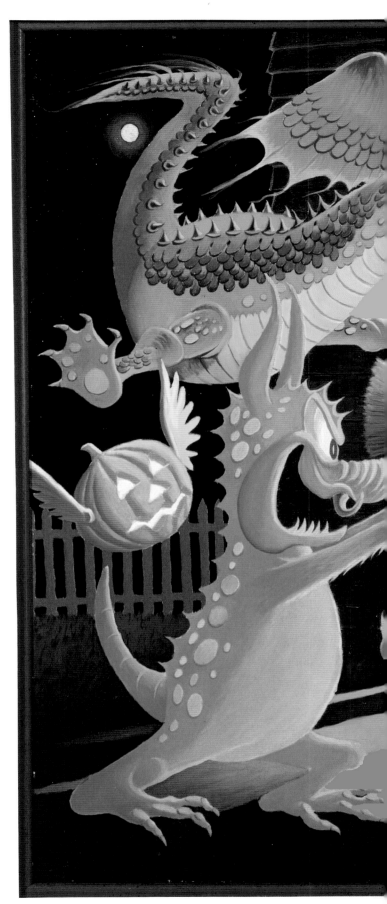

67   *Halloween in Duckburg,* 1973

CARL BARKS

© WALT DISNEY PRODUCTIONS

68   *The Prince and the Pauper*, story sketch, 1990

69

59

70

71

72

69–72   *The Prince and the Pauper*, rough animations, set of 4, 1990

77   *The Prince and the Pauper*, cel set-up, 1990

73–76   *The Prince and the Pauper*, clean-up animations, set of 4, 1990

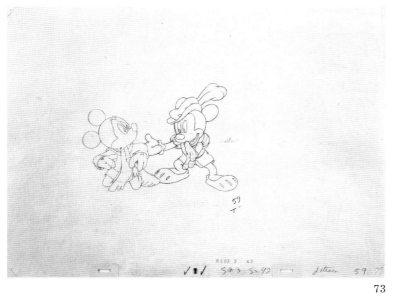

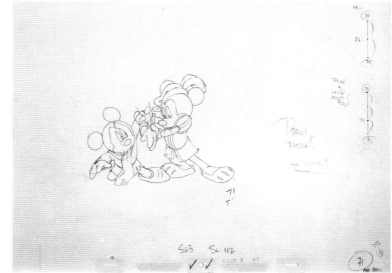

Andy's Enterprise: Nothing Special

by Dave Hickey

If everyone's not a beauty, then no one is.[1]

Andy Warhol

I

THE JOB AND THE WORK

[Emile de Antonio] was the first person I know of to see commercial art as real art and real art as commercial art.[2]

Andy Warhol / Pat Hackett

The poet's first job of work is to put bread on the table.[3]

Yvor Winters

This much is agreed upon: for good or ill, Andy Warhol changed the visual construction of the world we live in. By the time of his death in 1987 he was generally regarded, along with Pablo Picasso and Jackson Pollock, as one of the three most important artists of this century. He was also a working man, a social climber, an empire builder, an acquirer of goods, an effeminate homosexual and a radical Jacksonian democrat; and none of these appellations is insignificant in the consideration of his art. He was also the only major artist of this century possessed of "public spirit" as defined in its true eighteenth-century sense as "the Desire for Fame, or the Applause of Men, directed to the End of public Happiness."[4]

When one considers whence Warhol came, however, and with what, none of these attributes is particularly surprising, however amazing their consequences. He was born Andrew Warhola on August 6, 1928, the youngest son of Czechoslovakian immigrants Andrej and Julia Warhola, in Pittsburgh, Pennsylvania–at that time a smoky, blue-collar steel town on the cusp of the American midwest and on the brink of the Great Depres-

sion–an appropriately Dickensian setting, one may be sure, for a decidedly Dickensian childhood. And although later in life Warhol would pay homage to the plain-style and production-oriented work ethic of his birthplace by dubbing his Manhattan studio "The Factory," growing up there, sickly and impoverished, in a working-class ghetto on the wrong side of the tracks, young Andrew Warhola was anything but at home.

He was, in fact, easily as alienated from the rough factory culture of his home town as he would later feel himself to be from the strenuous, masculine painting culture of the New York Abstract Expressionists. So the factory was just the first of many institutions (from the Castelli gallery, to the international Jet Set, to the Museum of Modern Art) from which Warhol felt himself excluded, and into the midst of which he would ultimately–by guile, invention, and ironic legerdemain–translate himself.

In 1945, after an erratic and desultory public education, young Andrew Warhola was able, through his own and his family's diligent efforts, to enroll in the art curriculum at the Carnegie Institute of Technology. There, he and his classmate Phillip Pearlstein were befriended by Balcomb Greene, the American abstract painter and modernist critic whose refined, Apollonian view of the artist's vocation would ultimately provide the polar extreme against which Warhol's art would define itself. It was, in fact, one of Greene's much-quoted dismissals of didactic and socially conscious art that would, some seventeen years later, provide the ironic subtext for one of Warhol's most radical and infamous artistic gestures.

"Socially conscious art," Greene was fond of pointing out, always provided ludicrous instances of "the soap box speaking instead of the man."[5]

In 1964 Warhol would provide the world with just such an instance by filling the Stable Gallery with ranks of soap boxes–wooden blocks, suitable for standing upon, stencilled to resemble cases of Brillo soap pads–soap boxes, to be sure, speaking about a secular and egalitarian vision of the artist's vocation formulated on the streets of Pittsburgh.

By the summer of 1949, however, Andrew Warhola had finished with those streets. He graduated from Carnegie Institute with a degree in pictorial design and, in the company of his friend Pearlstein, he immediately moved to Manhattan. There he embarked upon a career as a commercial illustrator that would almost immediately bear fruit, and, although over the next ten years he would become the most influential and successful commercial illustrator in the city, he never for a moment ceased to take himself seriously.

Then, in 1960, Warhol began making paintings of comic strips, advertisements and consumer goods that differed as much from his own commercial work as they did from the fashionable painting of the day. In their eccentricity, these paintings make it clear that, however much Warhol might have wished to be "accepted" as a serious artist, he wanted most of all to be accepted on his own terms. He began making his Pop images, therefore, not as a commercial illustrator aspiring to become a serious artist, but as a serious artist aspiring to become a "major" artist by destroying the boundaries between "real art" and "commercial art" and reconstituting the whole historical endeavor in his own image.

Warhol would ultimately use these Pop images to mount an all-out assault upon the elite citadel of American high culture, which was at that time a virtual cult of heroic individualism and masculine self-expression and which, needless to say, couldn't have been less ready to destroy the boundaries between "real" art and "commercial" art. The Second World War was over and everyone was happy that it was, but there were a great many men in positions of power in America who were unwilling and unable to abandon the doomsday posturing that the war had made so fashionable.

Jackson Pollock, needless to say, defined American painting in this world, and *The Death of a Salesman* characterized its theater. (The death of salesmen, generally, was at this time a consummation devoutly to be wished.) Saul Bellow and Norman Mailer were the white hopes of its written word, and everywhere in the ivory towers of learning and on the pages of the learned magazines there was despair over America–over American television, American business, American movies, American cars, American music, and American suburbia and its tacky interior design. Entire careers, like those of Lewis Mumford, Dwight McDonald and Clement Greenberg, were built upon articulation of this despair.

The Barbarians were at the gate: Elvis was in Memphis, Buddy Holly was in Lubbock, Marilyn was in Hollywood, and Jack Kerouac was on the road between them. The Hucksters of Madison Avenue were using "hidden persuaders" to sell us things we weren't supposed to want, and *all* the young artists were worried about "selling out"–accidentally or on purpose. How could you tell? There were university seminars on the subject and teleplays about losing your soul to advertising on *Playhouse 90*. People even said that *Pollock* had "sold out" and had only partially redeemed himself by driving into a tree. They said that Kerouac had "sold out" and even Kerouac believed them. He immediately embarked upon a program of alcoholic hara-kiri.

The rank and file of culturally involved Americans, of course, were guilty of complicity in these "tragedies." Didn't they enable Kerouac's "sell-out" by purchasing his books? And "cheapen" Pollock's endeavor by reading about him in *Time Magazine?* Of course they did. But still, how *did* one become a hero without becoming celebrated and therefore a celebrity? And how *did* one make one's work public without getting "publicity"? And, if one put one's "self" into one's art, how did one sell it without selling one's "self"? And how, without "selling," did one put bread on the table? It was a real problem. Andy Warhol's future depended upon his devising a solution.

II[6]

THE PRINCE AND THE PRODUCT

Believe me ... I've made a career out of being the right thing in the wrong space and the wrong thing in the right space. That's one thing I really do know about.[7]
Andy Warhol

You should always have a product that has nothing to do with who you are or what people think about you ... so that you never start thinking that your product is you, or your fame or your aura.[8]
Andy Warhol

Andy Warhol was no theorist, but he was a *great* problem solver and his problem with American culture in the late 1950s was that a hugely successful, gay commercial illustrator who wanted to be a hugely successful "fine artist" hadn't a snowball's chance in hell of becoming one – because any image that he made would be defined by his "commerciality," his "success," and his "gayness." And these were "bad" words at that time. Unless he made them good, his ambitions were doomed. So, from the outset, Warhol was working from an understanding of the degree to which images are bound by context. He understood that they are

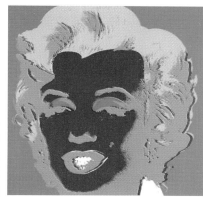

what they are, because of *where* they are, and *who* made them, and *how* their virtues are described in language.

This, I think, is the profound lesson that Warhol learned from the tragedy of Abstract Expressionism – the terrible lesson he learned from Jackson Pollock, which Pollock learned too late – that, even though a drip painting in his studio might have been an emblem of the seeking self, that same painting in a Connecticut summer home would be a background for gracious living. In a bank, it would become a metaphor for the intricacies of heroic commerce, and on the pages of *Life Magazine* it would become the symptomatic dribblings of a drunken madman. And he was helpless to prevent it. No matter what he might say or do, Clement Greenberg and Harold Rosenberg and Henry Luce were going to have the last say about what he had done.

Warhol learned from this, first, that you couldn't succeed with an art based on the idea of failure. If you were going to hang your work in the summer homes of Connecticut with no tinge of hypocrisy, you had better embrace success. Secondly, he learned that you couldn't succeed with works of art that could be dominated by their context. If you sent an image into a bank or a museum, you had to take strong measures to place it at odds with the values of those environments. Thirdly, he learned that if you intended to be a famous artist, you had best efface yourself in your work and in your life, as well. Otherwise something you might say could delimit the meaning of your work and, even if it didn't, that work would always be regarded as tinged with your fame and symptomatic of your "self" – better to be famous just for being famous and to make art on the side. And, finally, Warhol learned that one could not simply disre-

gard the language and the media that describe and reproduce works of art. One either submitted to that language and reproduction or subverted it.

Warhol's solution to the problem of submitting one's images to the context of summer homes, banks, museums, and critical discourse, of course, was simply to create images that were as much imposters as their creator. He would achieve visibility and maintain it by devising exactly the "wrong" image for the right place, and by accommodating his images to criticism in exactly the "wrong" way.[9] The problem with the media, of course, was easily solved. One simply stole one's imposter images *from* the media, so when the media stole them back, they simply disappeared into the mire from which they had come–the wrong image in the wrong place again.

If this seems a little too much like "deep thought" for Andy, look at it this way: Warhol, on the brink of his fine arts career, was a task-oriented professional. His job as a commercial illustrator was turning words into pictures in order to manipulate the aura of value around particular commodities. In the ad-parlance of the time, one didn't sell the steak, one "sold the sizzle," and it was Warhol's task to provide that sizzle. So it's not hard to imagine him looking at the products of the "high art" market of his time and thinking, "I don't mind the steak, but I *hate* the sizzle," and then setting out to extinguish that sizzle, not by attacking the paintings but by attempting to discredit the ad copy–the rhetoric of self-involved, mysto-mytho-macho catch phrases and slogans that invested them with value.

So he began, really, as any young artist would, by making images that accommodated themselves to the slogans and catch phrases of his time, but, as no other artist has ever done, he made them *exactly* wrong–and wrong, it should be noted, in exactly the same way. All of these early images, in one

way or another, "civilize" the appeal to the primitive that was then fashionable in critical discourse, and subvert its attribution of "personal" and psychological qualities to technique.

In his "Do It Yourself" paintings, for instance, Warhol presents us with a series of semi-completed paint-by-numbers canvases that sweetly misconstrue the canon of "unfinishedness" which, at that time, equated lack of *fini* with "self-expression" and treated incompletion as an existential metaphor for the artistic personality in the process of "becoming." He went on to misconstrue the inflated diction about mythological and archetypical womanhood that had accrued about de Kooning's paintings of women. Conflating the idea of "heroism" with "celebrity," as he always did, he offered up his blunt, stylized images of Elizabeth Taylor, Marilyn Monroe and the Mona Lisa. ("Like that?" he seems to say, in mock innocence. "Are these girls archetypal enough for you?")

He then proceeds to execute these images again and again, in different colors and formats, in a perfect travesty of the Abstract Expressionist penchant for obsessively reiterating the same pictorial idea in different chromatic circumstances. In the process, of course, Warhol suavely distinguishes the domains of "content" and "quality" (image and color) that are organically confounded in Abstract Expressionist pictures.

Into a context aglow with Rothko and Newman's quasi-religious musings about the possibilities of intra-subjective communication and redemption in the artist's struggle, Warhol blithely inserts his own "exactly wrong" images–of covert communication (Air Mail Stamps) and of redemption (S + H Green Stamps). Into the colloquy of learned discourse concerning Jackson Pollock's shamanistic ritual dance around the canvas, Andy plops these dumb "Dance Diagrams," more suited to the tootsies of Vernon Castle or Ramon Navarro than to those of the noble savage–making, in the process,

the rather shrewd semiotic point that so-called "paintings" made on the floor and hung on the wall are as much "pictures" as his diagrams (which were themselves originally shown on the floor). Then, having domesticated this neo-primitivist dance into cocktail Terpsichore, Warhol pastoralizes Pollock's "apocalyptic" wallpaper into a field of cows.

Later, in the 1970s, he would secularize and collectivize Pollock's drip paintings by having all of his friends urinate on oxidized canvas. In the light of Warhol's oft-expressed admiration for those paintings, however, this gesture should probably be taken as much in homage as in critique – Andy doing macho stuff, just like Jackson but with a better understanding of the situation.

III

THE POP AND THE ART

I used to drink it, I used to have the same lunch everyday, for twenty years, I guess, the same thing over and over again.[10]
Andy Warhol

If the critique of culture were all there were to these early works of Andy Warhol's, they would, of course, be far more Conceptual than Pop. And, probably, they wouldn't even be art. But Warhol's work is always as much about praise and tradition as it is about criticism. So we would make a serious mistake by supposing that Warhol's Marilyns and Mona Lisas, his dance diagrams and walls of Cows, didn't "mean" something to him. When asked, he would always say that "Pop Art is a way of liking things"[11] – encapsulating his strategy of celebration and critique into a double entendre. It was Andy's way of saying that Pop Art is always *two* things: that, first, it is a way of celebrating people and things and images, and, secondly, it is a way of "likening" them – of showing how they are

"alike." And, finally, of course, Pop Art is *art* and, as such, it enters into the discourse of a long tradition of images in a serious way.

So it is important for us to know that, although Brigid Berlin suggested it, Warhol himself *chose* to paint Campbell's soup cans because they "meant" something to him. He "liked" them in a simple and affectionate way, and it was that sentiment, as much as their "commercial" overtones, that made them profoundly "wrong" by the heroic standards of his time. They reminded him of his *mother,* for heaven's sake, and of quiet afternoons in Pittsburgh and New York, when she would heat him up a can of Campbell's.

But if this personal sentiment made the soup cans wrenchingly anti-heroic, the fact that they functioned for Warhol as private icons of mutability and domestic tranquility – recalling Cézanne's pipe or Peto's cup and cake – placed them firmly within a "still-life" tradition of domestic images that provided an ideal setting for his revolutionary strategy. A whole litany of artists, from Sanchez-Cotan to Chardin to Cézanne, from Peto and Harnett to Picasso and Braque, have resorted to this modest genre in their efforts to reform and reconstitute the nature of representation in their time.

Since the seventeenth century, in fact, still life has functioned as the classic transitional mode for anti-heroic, vanguard painting (and there was never an artist more vanguard nor more anti-heroic than Warhol, nor one more sensitive to tradition). Further, in the context in which they were first shown, these soup cans functioned as a subversive visual pun that more than reinforced Warhol's revisionist ideology.

That context, of course, was the early 1960s in New York when every second gallery wall seemed to be dripping with the viscous effluvia of Abstract Expressionism in its last mannerist swoon. At that time, the irreverent street slang for all this splash and dribble was "soup." So when you brought your friends off the street to see Warhol's pictures there was this little ritual. Someone would always take the role of the innocent. He would gaze about the gallery, as if lost, and, in mock confusion, exclaim, *"Where's the soup?"* And everyone else would respond in unison, *"In the cans!"*[12]

This was, in Factory argot, "getting it exactly wrong," by taking the "inside" and putting it "outside," and taking the "outside" and putting it "inside."[13] In this case, the commodity trademark logo, guaranteeing "originality," that was usually kept tastefully covert in gallery situations, was emblazoned shamelessly on the outside of the package, while the "soup" that most galleries seemed to be peddling that year was tidily tinned up. So, when Barbara Rose proclaimed her annoyance at having to see in a gallery what she was forced to look at in the supermarket, she was rather willfully missing the point.[14]

Warhol, after all, was forcing us to acknowledge that, despite its aspiration to "higher things," an art gallery was, indeed, a market – if not a supermarket, then at least a meta-market where, through the sublimation of appetite, we concern ourselves with commodities in good taste rather than commodities that taste good. Taken together, then, Warhol's aggregation of soup can images provides us with what amounts to an entry-level course in the uneasy relationship between consumption and connoisseurship.

These remedial lessons were nowhere better taught than at Warhol's first one-man show at the Ferus Gallery in Los Angeles. Thirty-two paintings of individual soup cans lined the walls of this exhibition, each labeled with a different flavor of soup, so that, having been reassured by the "originality" of the brand name on the label, one was free to select one's particular flavor according to

"taste" – just as one might do with "real" art. (Pop Art is a way of liking things and of showing that they are alike.)

The subsequent images in the soup can series extend this loopy analogy between works of art and cans of soup by addressing issues of "content" and "style." The images of soup cans with their labels torn away to reveal the bare can and the images of soup cans being attacked by can openers present us with bathetic metaphors for critical efforts at "ripping the lid off" to get "beneath the surface" to the real "inside content" of the work. The "fauve soup cans," on the other hand, abandon the quest for content in favor of a "developing style." In these images the trademark format and the labeled flavors remain constant – while the colors undergo elaborate and extravagant permutations, achieving striking "formal solutions" in a successful parody of modernist "artistic development."

Today, of course, the parody is unnecessary, and although the outrage and affection in these images remain fresh, their subversive subtexts have taken on a historical flavor – thanks in part to their own power and acuity. This means that the world has changed.

IV

THE DANDY AND THE DEMOCRAT

Once you "got" Pop, you could never see a sign the same way again.[15]   Andy Warhol/Pat Hackett

So, that much is agreed upon: for good or ill, Andy Warhol changed the world. He did so by making us conscious of the social bondage in which our vision languished. It is therefore important to remember that, for a while at least, the pre-Warhol and the post-Warhol world *looked* exactly the same – that

the objects and images in Warhol's art were there to be seen for a generation before he showed them to us. They comprised the visual vocabulary of Warhol's childhood – and that of a great many other Americans as well. Even so, it is impossible to look back and re-imagine the world before Warhol, even for those of us who grew up in the midst of it, because, although the materials of his art were visually available to us then, they were culturally invisible, and in the act of showing them to us as culture, Warhol restructured our vision of the past in a way from which there is no going back.

The eerie analogies between the two-tone soup can, the two-tone Chevy, and the two-tone Rothko will always be there now, as part of our visual intelligence, as will the connections between the Madonnas of the past and Warhol's Magdalenes of the future – his Marilyns and Lizzes. And these connections will never let us forget that, in our culture, images sell the commodities that their patrons want sold – soups, dreams, formal values, religious doctrines – and that the less we acknowledge these ideological commodities the more likely we are to buy into them. So, even the image that celebrates its own narcissistic formal autonomy, in Warhol's aesthetic, is only advertising its disdain for the beholder while hypocritically selling itself to him in the process.

So Warhol did not change the "look" of the images we see. He changed the way we look at them, the importance we attach to them, the power we attribute to them, and the similarities we see between them. For Warhol, though, this visual revisionism was not a matter of cultural altruism, it was a matter of survival. Confronted by a culture whose expressive priorities and primitivist, frontier values marginalized him as a human being and trivialized him as an artist, he had no choice,

really, but to rewrite its subtext "according to Andy."

In the light of his own common sense and his sense of self-worth, Warhol would apply to the world he found wanting what structural anthropologists now call "the principle of reversibility." His entire aesthetic language (which is also his social language and his political language) pivots around this idea of reversing content and context in order to generate a dynamic of transgression and inappropriateness. "Pop art took the inside and put it outside, took the outside and put it inside," he would say, making no distinction between the social and aesthetic senses of "inside" and "outside" – because for him there was none.

As a serious artist in a democracy riddled by exclusion, he could get it right only by "getting it exactly wrong." So he was always trying to get the "wrong" person for the "right" part, to put the "wrong" thing in the "right" space, to find the "wrong" image for the "right" word, or vice versa, because the consequence of all these reversals was democracy. It manifested itself in the equation of apparent antinomies – "Commercial art as real art, and real art as commercial art"[16] – and in the flattening of hierarchies: "I sat at Le Club one night staring at Jackie Kennedy, who was there in a black chiffon dress down to the floor, with her hair done by Kenneth – thinking how great it was that hairdressers were now going to dinner at the White House."[17]

V

THE AFTER AND THE BEFORE

When I think what sort of person I would most like to have on retainer, I think it would be a boss.[18]

Andy Warhol

*[Henry Geldzahler] liked to compare our relation-
ship to the Renaissance painters and the scholars
of mythology or antiquity or Christian history who
doled out the ideas for their subjects.*[19]

Andy Warhol/Pat Hackett

*Another time [Ivan Karp] said, "Why don't you
paint some cows, they're so wonderfully pastoral
and such a durable image in the history of the
arts." (Ivan talked like this.)*[20]　Andy Warhol/Pat Hackett

The amazing thing, finally, about
Andy Warhol's career is the extent
to which he was able to establish
his enterprise as an independent
and equal player among the cultural institutions of the 1970s and
1980s. By the end he was nothing
less than an artfully designed con-
glomerate beneath whose umbrella
he functioned at one time or an-
other as an avant-garde artist, a society portrait
painter, an author, a film-maker, a television host,
a nightclub owner, a record producer, a band
manager, a theatrical producer, a magazine pub-
lisher, a film actor and a fashion model.

"My style was always to spread out," he would say,
"rather than to move up."[21] And somehow in the
process of spreading out, he managed to maneuver
himself into a position of such mysterious authority that he could take suggestions from everyone while taking orders from no one, and make
suggestions to anyone while issuing orders to no
one. Further, he would use the unavoidable seman-
tic slippage involved in this process of nuance and
suggestion as a generative artistic device–as an
externalization, really, of Harold Bloom's model
for the "anxiety of influence."

For Warhol, it worked like this: He began by
asking everyone he knew what they thought he
should do, until, finally, he would hear one word,

or maybe misunderstand someone, and that would
put him onto a "good idea" of his own. At this
point he would delegate large portions of this new
task to an assistant by giving him general suggestions that, hopefully, would be "misunderstood" as
well, and in an interesting way, thus providing the
artist further "good ideas" of his own to enliven
his completion of the work, which would then
issue forth from the studio, hopefully, to be misunderstood by the citizens of the republic.

Warhol called this procedure "working from the outside,"[22] and it en-
abled him to externalize the entire
creative process–to transform it
into a systematic sequence of trans-
actions that encouraged "creative
accidents," and over which he exer-
cised absolute executive control.
Not surprisingly, the cultural consequences of this procedure have
been as interesting as its products.
First, the incrementally collaborative nature of
this process, with its inevitable and subversive
accommodation of public taste, has doubtless contributed mightily to the proliferation of Warhol's
influence.

On the other hand, this same collaborative process
has seriously confused and compromised the cultural discourse about Warhol's enterprise–laying
bare, in the process, the covert auteurist notions
that still underpin such discourse. Cultural com-
mentators, it would seem, regardless of their
decentrist proclamations, still like to speak with
authority *about* authority and the question of authority in Warhol's work is seriously compromised
on the authority of its author. There is always that
nagging question: if Leo and Bruno commissioned
the paintings, and Ivan and Henry suggested their
subject matter, and Ronnie and Gerard painted the
paintings, and Pat and Bob wrote the books, and
Paul made the movies, what did Andy *do*?

What he did, I would suggest, is to create the possibility of a post-modernist future by making visible in the modernist present the invisible cultural heritage of the pre-modern past. In other words, Warhol re-invigorated the conditions of patronage and consultation that governed art-making procedures in the west from the sixteenth through the eighteenth century – and then remained covertly in place for 150 years under the cloak of romantic and classical modernism. The sixteenth-century

master accepts a commission from his patron, negotiates a cost-plus deal with his patron's lawyer, consults with adjacent scholars and clergy over niceties of content and iconography. Then he executes a painting which, if it is a good painting, both embodies and subverts the values of the institutions that sanction it and without which it could not exist at all as a part of the cultural discourse. You can almost hear Warhol saying (or Fred Hughes saying for him): *"Quelle différence!"*.

The only difference, really, is that contemporary artists in our time work largely on spec – soliciting institutional sanction after the fact, and consulting with the culture by clandestine means. "How is asking people for ideas any different from looking for them in a magazine?" Andy would ask.[23] The answer, of course, is that looking for ideas in a magazine enables one to maintain the romantic fiction of "autonomy" and "originality"; and Warhol did a lot of things, but he did *not* do fiction. If he felt the need of a patron, a consultant, a confidant, he would recruit one – or a hundred – flinging open the doors of his studio, transforming that traditional romantic garret, that "cathedral of the

self," into a confluence of the "other" – a rough and ready salon of street trash and courtiers after the manner of the good-hearted Boucher who, like Warhol, collected people and precious stones and genuinely enjoyed his work.

The difference, of course, is that Warhol was a democrat; he sought to reform the institutions of privilege whose favor he courted. By designing cognitive insecurity, mischance, and misunderstanding into his procedures, he strove to get it "exactly wrong" and then, by force of will, to make that "wrong" right.

The fact remains, however, that Warhol's post-modern accommodation of the pre-modern past has, to a large extent, restored that past to us. Without the dark modernist glaze of romantic individualism or the exclusive mod-ernist teleology of progress toward abstraction, we can see it now – in all its argumentative glamor – as a part of the same never-ending, noisy discourse, the same rough dance of culture at which we now stand in attendance.

The emblem of this "new" past, restored to us – scraped of its dark modernist glaze – now floats above the Sistine Chapel: and gazing up at it, beholding it in all of its rhetorical dazzle, in all of its high-intensity, cartoony inappropriateness, it's hard to believe that we should ever have seen it were it not for Andy showing us a world in which such things can happen. We would have missed a breathtaking and confusing spectacle, to be sure.

And we would have missed, as well, a new Michelangelo – one more like Andy than Jackson – kicking out the stops on a commissioned project, and a new Pope Julius – one more like Bob Scull than Rex Harrison – standing on the floor shouting up at the artist on the scaffolding, "It's great, Mike! Just great! But can't you make it *brighter?*" Just the kind of boss Andy would have loved to put on retainer.

78   *The Men in her Life (Mike Todd and Eddie Fisher)*, 1962 & 1978

79   *Warren*, 1962

80 *Troy*, 1962–63

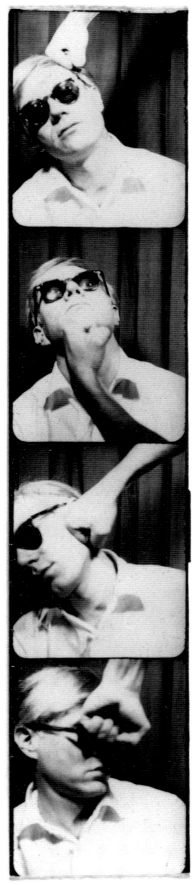

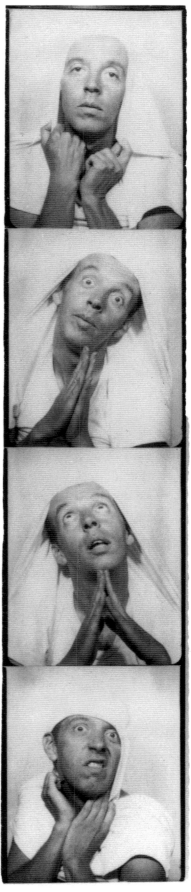

81 *Andy Warhol*, 1963   82 *Ethel Scull*, 1963   84 *Taylor Mead*, c. 1966

85   *Edie Sedgwick, c.* 1966   86   *Unidentified (Jackson Browne?),*   90   *Sandra Brant,* 1968
                                                 c. 1966

83 *Jacqueline Kennedy,* 1964

87 *Marilyn*, 1967

87 *Marilyn*, 1967

87   *Marilyn*, 1967

87   *Marilyn*, 1967

87   *Marilyn*, 1967

87   *Marilyn*, 1967

87   *Marilyn*, 1967

88   *Self-Portrait*, 1967

89   *Untitled (Campbell's Soup Can)*, 1967

91   *Kellogg's Boxes (Corn Flakes)*, 1971

92   Mao Tse-Tung, 1972

93   *Mao Tse-Tung*, 1972

94   *Mao Tse-Tung*, 1972

95   *Brooke Shields*, 1976–86

96 *The Marx Brothers* from the portfolio *Ten Portraits of Jews of the Twentieth Century*, 1980

97   *Joseph Beuys, State III, 1980/83*

98   *Myths: Mickey Mouse*, 1981

99   *The Star (Garbo)* from the portfolio *Myths*, 1981

100   *Uncle Sam* from the portfolio *Myths*, 1981

101   *Superman* from the portfolio *Myths*, 1981

102   *The Witch* from the portfolio *Myths*, 1981

103 *Mammy* from the portfolio *Myths*, 1981

104   *Howdy Doody* from the portfolio *Myths*, 1981

105   *Dracula* from the portfolio *Myths*, 1981

106   *Mickey Mouse* from the portfolio *Myths*, 1981

107   *Santa Claus* from the portfolio *Myths*, 1981

108   *The Shadow* from the portfolio *Myths*, 1981

99–108 *Myths*, 1981

109   *Portrait of Keith Haring and Juan Dubose, 1983*

110 *Portrait of Keith Haring and Juan Dubose, 1984*

111   *Grace Kelly*, 1984

112   *Blackglama (Judy Garland)* from the portfolio *Ads*, 1985

113   *Rebel Without a Cause (James Dean)* from the portfolio *Ads*, 1985

114   *Van Heusen (Ronald Reagan)* from the portfolio *Ads*, 1985

115   *The New Spirit (Donald Duck)* from the portfolio *Ads*, 1985

116   *Anniversary Donald Duck*, 1985

117   *Dolly Parton*, 1985

118 *Dolly Parton*, 1985

DANCY
NANCY
K. Haring™

The Radiant Child (Keith Haring)

by Bruce D. Kurtz

The Radiant Child on the button is Haring's Tag. It is a slick Madison Avenue colophon. It looks as if it's always been there. The greatest thing is to come up with something so good it seems as if it's always been there, like a proverb.[1]

When the poet Rene Ricard named Keith Haring's image of the crawling baby the "Radiant Child" (catalogue number 194), the verbal image seemed as apt as the visual one. The lines radiating from the baby indicate spiritual light glowing from within, as though the baby were a holy figure from a religious painting, only the glow is rendered in the visual vocabulary of a cartoon. That is what makes it so universally comprehensible and, to face the issue squarely, culturally suspect, at least by some of the guardians of high art. The learned art historical references, such as they are, are couched in the common visual language of popular art.

Haring's Radiant Child signals hope and possibility. It symbolizes the sense of renewal that a new life brings, along with the feeling of openness and freedom from pre-judgments that typify children, qualities that Haring constantly renewed in himself through contact with children and young people.

Haring's Radiant Child is an idealized self-portrait. It first became widely known in the artist's subway drawings and then turned into a button that he had made in the thousands and gave away to people who recognized him in the subway, on the streets, or in the clubs he frequented. The Radiant Child does not represent Haring's entire persona, not the person who made images indicting nuclear weapons, apartheid, drugs, AIDS, unsafe sex, and other social ills; or the sexually liberated young gay man who made hundreds of explicit, homoerotic images. But it represents a universal spirit that was at the core of his being and that transcends gender, sexual orientation, race, and politics. The spirit of the Radiant Child typifies the works that were selected for this exhibition, works that reveal many of Haring's affinities with Warhol and Disney.

The Radiant Child became a "colophon" and a "proverb" because it stands for something simple and honest that was possible to believe in, even for jaded New Yorkers in 1981. Haring's small-town-boy naivety, combined with his overreaching ambition and brilliant intuition of how mass media work, represented the dream of every kid coming to New York for their shot at the big time. The Radiant Child represents the lovable possibility of making a place for oneself in the world.

Drawing Lines   The basis of Haring's art is the drawn line that he constantly and restlessly practiced beginning when he was a very young child and his father drew cartoons with him at the kitchen table. Haring's first lesson in the socially enfranchising power of art came when his schoolmates looked up to him for his cartooning ability. As a young commercial art student (briefly) in Pittsburgh in 1976, where he first became aware of the work of Pierre Alechinsky, Jean Dubuffet, and Fernand Léger (at the Carnegie Museum of Art), Haring was struck by their use of cartoon-like images and their apparent spontaneity, which gave artistic pedigree to his already widely practiced, free-flowing line.

1978–79 found Haring at the School of Visual Arts in New York City, where he began his exposure to the automatic writing of Dada and surrealism - the practice of letting the hand and mind wander, allowing "accidents" to happen – and to the Abstract Expressionists' adoption of automatism, especially by Mark Tobey and Jackson Pollock. Pollock's allover composition – the idea of his paintings having no distinct beginning or end but instead being a continuum where every visual incident is of equal interest – also struck Haring as

one of the many ideas he could apply to his own art.

The important thing is not so much what Haring borrowed from whom as what he did with it. Haring linked what he learned from fine artists with what he knew about line from the popular art of cartoons and what he was about to discover in the folk art of graffiti. Haring's was the comprehensive imagination of a self-taught artist who refused to compartmentalize ideas according to conventional categories. Instead, he synthesized elements from wide-ranging sources into his own vision.

The late 1970s and early 1980s were a time when graffiti were very much in evidence in the New York subways. Whole trains were covered inside and out with spray-painted and magic-markered images, many of them showing remarkable graphic wit and sophistication. Haring admired the immediate visual impact the images had, their visual velocity. Not only were they painted at high speed (to avoid arrest) but they were designed to be seen while the trains were in motion as well as stopped at the stations. Covering entire trains, they seemed a grass-roots extension of Pollock's allover composition overlaid on the excitement of everyday visual life.

From the Conceptual Art of the 1960s, which largely comprised his curriculum at the School of Visual Arts, Haring learned the importance of *context* for visual art. A dictionary definition printed on canvas by Joseph Kosuth and exhibited in an art gallery became art because of the context in which it was presented. Thanks to Conceptual Art's precedent, post-modernists used language-as-art outside of art's normal context. Jenny Holzer began pasting up her posters listing numerous *Truisms,* like "A Strong Sense of Duty Imprisons You" and "Calm is More Conducive to Creativity Than is Anxiety," on out-

door walls in the late 1970s. Around this same time, the "street artist" Richard Hambleton painted threatening, shadowy figures directly on doorways and dark walls all over Manhattan. The moment was ripe with the possibility of making art outside galleries and museums, art that was partly about its context.

The chalk drawings that Haring began making in the New York subways in 1981 first matched his imagery with exactly the right context for it. The Metropolitan Transportation Authority's brief practice of covering advertising posters with black paper when their rental time expired presented the *tabula rasa* for his graffiti-alerted, Conceptual art-minded, *art brut,* COBRA, and Abstract Expressionist-informed, cartoon-loving *horror vacui* to seize upon.

Haring's already high-velocity lines gained greater momentum by his having to draw them quickly to avoid arrest. Even so, he was given summonses more than 100 times by his count. His physical movements and the energy they embodied flowed into his lines. After hundreds of the drawings appeared (and kept coming for five years), people stopped on the subway platforms to watch him draw, like a kind of performer. This is when he started giving away the buttons of the Radiant Child.

The movement and energy that the subway drawings helped Haring's line to evolve also came from his lifelong involvement with music. He hardly ever worked without listening to music. He tried to arrange his travel schedule to allow him to be in New York on Saturday nights so he could go to the Paradise Garage or other clubs where he listened to music, danced, and mixed with the racially and economically diverse young crowd that fed him so much energy. The clubs were a great place for social leveling, where everyone was only as good as the energy they put out. Music – its rhythms, repetitions, movement, cadence, syncopation, and energy – is almost audible in Haring's line.

The speed that Haring's lines embody is not only the quickness of his actual drawing time but also a function of their tensile strength and resilience. The lines feel like taut bars of metal temporarily coaxed into the position from which they could spring at any moment. Their resilience makes them seem endowed with a life force. The lines' speed gives Haring's images a declaratory insistence that allows them to be quickly apprehended at a glance.

Around the time of the early subway chalk drawings, Haring combined a naive notion of allover composition with the *horror vacui* of graffiti artists and a childlike desire to make marks on whatever surface presented itself: he painted "all over" a *Headboard* (catalogue number 121), *A Pair of Corinthian Columns* (with L.A. II, catalogue number 120), *Skateboards* (catalogue numbers 134 – 36), and numerous other pre-existing objects. "The way I'm making art," Haring said, "is a lot closer to the way it was in primitive cultures, when art was everywhere, on people's houses, on their tools, on their bodies, when art was part of the ritual of daily life instead of something to put on a pedestal in museums."[2]

Mass Media and Popular Culture   When Haring took his leave from the Phoenix Art Museum in 1986, a young woman who was then a member of our staff squealed, "He kissed me with the same lips that kissed Madonna!" By then he was as famous as a rock star. "Andy [Warhol] was the first artist to really take it to the extent where his image was his art. That was one of the things that I inherited from him or followed through with him because the same thing happened to me, almost without trying."[3]

Haring's fame grew out of the mass-media coverage that exhalted the artist as much as his art. The art critic David Galloway alluded to the merging of art and artist when he wrote: "Leslie Fiedler once referred to Huck [Mark Twain's *Huckleberry Finn*] as the 'good bad boy' of American culture–a type who appears to flaunt all social conventions but who affirms, in the end, the rich resources of the human spirit. By using the voice of a child, Twain plumbed the contradictory depths of his society; he composed a tragic book full of laughter and celebration. Keith Haring had much in common with Huck–including the latter's small-town background, his moral vision, his generosity, his holistic yearnings, his sense of mischief, his distrust of bourgeois pretensions, his openness to experience, his questing spirit. Keith, like Huck, was an American voyager."[4]

Like some authors for whom their fictional characters become surrogate selves, Haring was a performer in his own art.[5] His personality and his mass-media image were so thoroughly identified with his art that they became one and the same thing. "So much of what I do has to do with performance, because of the way I paint, because of traveling. I try to do things around the whole world. That plan has made me become a kind of–almost like a rock star that's on tour."[6] "It's a whole different role, and I'm inventing the role as I go along."[7]

The first widespread dissemination of Haring's art into popular culture and the mass media took place with the subway drawings.[8] The images in the subway drawings turned up all over the world soon after Haring first drew them, even before he had his first show in an art gallery in 1982. They were copied and changed and appeared on T-shirts, dresses, sneakers, and posters in Thailand, Brazil, Japan, Australia, and other places

from jungles to third world and industrialized countries.

Most of Haring's figures are without gender, race, age (except the Radiant Child), or even facial features. They represent humankind, not men or women, not whites or blacks, Hispanics, Asians, or Native Americans, not adults, the elderly, or children, but everyone. Both by their content and by their design, Haring's images are inherently capable of being almost instantly transmitted around the world. "Living in 1984, the role of the artist has to be different from what it was fifty, or even twenty years ago. I am continually amazed at the number of artists who continue working as if the camera were never invented, as if Andy Warhol never existed, as if airplanes and computers and videotape were never heard of."[9]

By Haring's estimate the subway drawings numbered about 5,000 over the five years that he made them (from 1980 to 1985). He believed that they were his most important work. In his last interview Haring said "There is nothing you can criticize about it because I was doing it purely for the love of doing it and for the love of drawing and for the love of the people that were seeing it.... I don't think that since then I've ever done anything as pure as that.... I think it's the most important thing I ever did."[10]

The subway drawings set the tone for the rest of Haring's career. Installations of his art outside the subways often maintained the visual complexity of the subway context. For its showing of *Keith Haring, Andy Warhol, and Walt Disney*, the Phoenix Art Museum installed Haring's art the way he preferred it to be seen (see installation views on page 23). Hanging the artworks against brightly colored walls in groupings resembles the display methods used for advertising and merchandise more than the white walls and even spacing of conventional contemporary fine art installations. This is the method Haring used for his first gallery show at the Tony Shafrazi Gallery in 1982 and for most subsequent exhibitions.

The sociopolitical ramifications of how his art is presented – its context – are part of Haring's content. His art's aggressiveness and quick take seem almost overbearing in the neutral viewing space of a gallery or museum where visual distractions are normally minimized, where instead of the more democratic everything-at-once visual melee of urban streets an aura of visual privilege usually prevails. "The subway drawings opened my eyes to this whole other understanding of art as something that really could have an effect on and communicate to larger numbers of people that were increasingly becoming the harbors of the art.... [Art was] used as a way of separating the general population from the upper class ... I think those barriers started being broken down by Madison Avenue advertising, television, and Andy Warhol, but there's still a really long way to go."[11]

Jazz Though Haring's art achieved widespread popular recognition very early in his career, the art establishment was slow to acknowledge it. Something similar happened to jazz. Jazz was popularly accepted as an artistic development long before the intelligentsia recognized it as being one of America's greatest contributions to music, along with the blues and rock and roll. The role of improvisation and of the solo performance in both jazz and Haring's art are striking similarities. Haring said he drew "without a pre-determined plan or concept,"[12] improvising like a jazz musician. But the associations of jazz and Haring's art with lower-class racial minorities and culturally

unhallowed spaces like nightclubs are more likely reasons for their critical neglect.

Graffiti appealed to Haring partly because they are the grass-roots visual imagery of racially mixed lower-class urban kids. Having grown up drawing cartoons–perhaps the white, suburban, middle-class equivalent of graffiti–Haring felt an affinity for the urban relation.

Racial politics were the root of New York graffiti in the early 1980s. The kids who wrote on the trains were mostly blacks and Hispanics from the ghettoes whose access to mainstream culture was completely cut off. Haring took his cue from them in using the streets and subways as a way to put his art before the public. For a few years in the early 1980s, a small number of graffiti artists showed their work in galleries, but their imagery could not make the transition into a fine art context. Haring, who understood the significance of context for visual imagery, and who never was a graffiti artist to begin with, successfully placed his imagery in three contexts: those of folk art (graffiti), popular art (mass-media imagery), and fine art.

The lower-class connotations of folk art and the middle-class aversion to accepting popular art as serious imagery combined with the association of graffiti with blacks, Hispanics, and vandalism to cause the mostly white, upper-middle to upper-class critical apparatus of the fine art world to hesitate in accepting Haring's art, just as the same apparatus initially balked at accepting jazz for similar reasons.

Jazz made the status transition from low-class popular entertainment to high-class art in Europe before the United States. Haring's earliest critical acclaim and museum exhibitions took place in Europe, in 1985 at the Musée d'Art Contemporain in Bordeaux and in 1985–86 at one of Europe's most prestigious contemporary art venues, the Stedelijk Museum in Amsterdam. Until our current exhibition, these European venues presented his most noteworthy museum shows.

Some Murals   By 1986 Haring had ceased to draw in the subways. No sooner did he make the drawings than someone tore them off the wall, and they started showing up framed in trendy lofts, where Haring had never intended them to be seen. The subway drawings engendered another form of public visual declaration: murals. Like the subway drawings, Haring made most of the murals free of charge, painting them as a gift to the public.

With the help of his friend Juan Du Bose (depicted with Haring in Warhol's two *Portrait*(s) *of Keith Haring and Juan Du Bose* [catalogue numbers 109 and 110], Haring painted one of his earliest murals in 1982 on a 15 x 50-foot freestanding wall facing Houston and Bowery Streets, on the fringe of SoHo. It included two images of the three-eyed smiling face (catalogue number 122), running figures, and symbols of the atomic age.

In June 1986 Haring painted *Crack is Wack* on an abandoned handball court at East Harlem Drive and 128th Street in Manhattan. He just showed up one day with ladders and paints and completed the mural in one day without permission. His motivation was very personal: his studio assistant, a bright and responsible Puerto Rican boy with medical-school ambitions, became addicted to crack. The boy eventually got into a detoxification program and was cured, but Haring was very moved by his struggle.

In October 1986 the Berlin Wall became Haring's ground for a 350-foot-long mural in the colors of the German flag (yellow, red, and black) depicting figures interlocking at their hands and feet "representing the unity of people as against the idea of

LIL' ANGEL
©K. Haring 89

147

the wall."[13] In the tradition of the Wall, by the next day other artists began painting over what Haring had done.

December of 1986 found Haring in Phoenix where he painted an 11 x 160-foot mural with 25 students from the city's pilot art program at South Mountain High School (pages 152–153). Since I was the local contact, I spent the five days of his visit with Haring, observing first hand the performance aspect of his art, his ability to communicate through the mass media, and his completely disarming sincerity.

People who met Haring, even only on a casual basis, were moved by how much he loved children and young people. Haring speculated that perhaps this was because his youngest sister, Kristen, was born when he was twelve years old, and he spent a lot of time with her when she was growing up. Whatever the origin of Haring's ability to communicate with young people, the high-school students who worked with him on the mural still recall it as the highlight of their lives.

Haring started painting the black outlines of the *Phoenix Mural* at about eleven o'clock in the morning, working from one end with a large brush, as usual without any preparatory drawings. By two-thirty in the afternoon he had reached the other end of the 11 x 160-foot mural. Twenty-five kids clamoring around, a large battery-operated boom box blasting music, passers-by stopping to make comments, media people asking questions and taking photographs–all of this activity sparked his energy. Following right behind him, the kids started filling in between the lines with their imagery.

The black outlines hold the various elements together, like a medieval stained-glass window or a coloring book. The mural became a statement of faith in Phoenix, a public declaration of confidence in the next generation and of renewal of a transitional block of downtown (the plywood panels board up windows of a store slated for demolition). It was the focus of a festival of good feelings and high spirits in the media and the populace at large, qualities that Haring fostered throughout his art and life. Art events that elicit such widespread public celebration are rare in contemporary America.

Haring's *Phoenix Mural* was intended as a performance art event as much as an art object. Still, it has lasted longer than anyone expected: though made of impermanent materials and intended to be temporary, it remains in place after more than five years.

Haring repeated the experiment of working with school kids in 1989 when he painted a 520-foot plywood mural with 300 kids from every high school in Chicago.

Paintings and Sculptures   Until 1982 Haring only made drawings and one mural, but in his first show at the Tony Shafrazi Gallery he wanted to show paintings too.

"...for the show I wanted to do some big paintings, which I had resisted doing all along. The reason was that I had an aversion to canvas. I always felt I would be impeded by canvas, because canvas seemed to have a certain value before you even touched it. I felt I wouldn't be free, the way I was working on paper–because paper was unpretentious and totally available and wasn't all that expensive. Also, for me, canvas represented this whole historical thing–and it just psychologically blocked me.

One day, I observed some Con Edison men working on the street, and they were covering their equipment with these vinyl tarpaulins, which had these little metal grommets in them. So I went up and inspected them and wanted to buy some of these tarpaulins. Well, I located a place in Brooklyn

CAT HAT
K. Haring™

called the Acme Rope and Canvas Company, which I partly chose because in Bugs Bunny cartoons, whenever Bugs Bunny has to get a product, it's made by Acme!"[14]

Haring's reluctance to use the art historically hallowed painting support of canvas recalls a remark that the art dealer Ambrose Vollard reported the French Impressionist Edgar Degas to have made. Degas, who did not cast any of his wax sculptures in bronze during his lifetime, said "There is too much responsibility in leaving behind something in bronze, this material for eternity."[15] Haring apparently felt the same way about canvas.

Evading historical allusions associates Haring's art with the present, the time frame of popular culture and mass-media imagery. It was partly a social class imperative with Haring, who studiously avoided doing anything that would alienate his working-class audience. More than anything at this point, he wanted the respect of the graffiti writers whose territory he had made part of his own. He wanted them not to feel that he was ripping them off. The tarpaulins that Haring chose to paint on have a working-class association, and their being made by Acme à la Bugs Bunny was just icing on the cake.

By 1985 Haring was no longer intimidated by canvas. "I decide to stop making tarpaulins. I no longer feel inhibited about using canvas, because I now have the money to buy it as though it were paper."[16] The occasion was a two-gallery exhibition of paintings and sculptures at the Tony Shafrazi Gallery and Leo Castelli's mammoth Greene Street gallery. "Having my sculptures at the Castelli Gallery really blows me away because … well, it's like this holy space!"[17]

"I decide to paint cartoon characters all around the walls of the [Castelli] gallery. It was the first time I introduced cartoon characters into a 'serious' art context. The figures are based on cartoons I made from the ages of ten to sixteen. But now, because my drawing ability is more advanced and sophisticated, I introduce these characters as art."[18]

Andy Mouse (catalogue number 126) dates from the first year Haring started painting on canvas. Along with the three Andy Mouse drawings in our exhibition (catalogue numbers 130, 133, and 140) and the two Andy Mouse prints (catalogue numbers 131 and 132), the painting pays homage to Haring's dual heroes, Andy Warhol and Walt Disney. The historically sanctioned fine-art medium of paint on canvas bears the images of two pop icons blended into one.

The Andy Mouse images may be idealized self-portraits, the second major ones since the Radiant Child, only now Haring is not as nascent as he once was; he's the mature product of the two pop icons who were his heroes. (If this seems egotistical, witness the 1989 Self-Portrait from a Portfolio of 8 Self-Portraits (catalogue number 178) which mockingly depicts Haring with big ears and a receding hairline.)

The drawing Untitled (Mickey Mouse) (catalogue number 119) dates from 1981, the year that Haring started the subway chalk drawings and two years after he left the School of Visual Arts. "The Mickey Mouse figure came out of drawing Mickey Mouse a lot when I was little. I've appreciated this anew because the drawings I'm doing now have more to do with what I drew in high school than with anything I did in art school. I did it partly because I could draw it so well and partly because it's such a loaded image. It's ultimately a symbol of America more than anything else."[19] He felt the same way about Warhol; about his Money Magazine "Andy Mouse Bill" (catalogue number 133) Haring said: "It's treating him [Warhol] like he was part of American culture, like Mickey Mouse was."[20]

The historically revered medium of paint on canvas did not intimidate Haring too much for him irreverently to paint the world's most ubiquitous cartoon character on it, returning more to what he remembered as a kid than utilizing his art school training, any more than the hallowed space of the Leo Castelli gallery intimidated him from filling it with cartoon characters. Haring maintained a proletarian edge despite his rising status, an edge he never abandoned.

Cartoon-like images rendered with Haring's characteristic animated lines were at first jarring in paint on canvas. But Haring knew from his early exposure to Alechinsky, Dubuffet, Léger, Picasso, and the Pop artists that it was possible to make a fine art statement using the common imagery of everyday life – that, in fact, the use of a common visual language would make his fine art more legible to the uninitiated audience he always sought to reach. Haring went beyond the art historical precedents to be more blatantly cartoon-like and childlike than any fine artist before him.

In 1991 it is difficult to rekindle the sense of bewilderment and possibility that greeted these first paintings on canvas – bewilderment to find a visual language derived from a blend of street art, cartoons, and paintings, made by a mass-media celebrity, painted on the sanctioned material of canvas, and shown in an art gallery. They embodied the possibility that the social class distinctions between fine art (upper class), popular art (middle class) and folk art (lower class) could be broken down; that the inequities of the races inherent in the class structure of visual imagery could be overturned; and that a young person making images in the visual language of youth could make art of consequence. This democratic equalization

FUNNY
BUNNY
K. Haring™

seemed to be the preposterously fresh possibility of a naive art world outsider.

When a reporter asked him in 1985 why he made the subway drawings, Haring said "It was easier to ... go directly to the audience."[21] He went "directly to the audience" with the visual language shared by mass media and certain contemporary fine art: exaggeration, overstatement, simplification, and the quick take.

Exaggeration and overstatement typify both the Neo-Expressionist painting and sculpture that emerged in the late 1970s and advertising imagery. The idea of simplifying a visual image to its most essential components has been central to both mass-media imagery and modern fine art since the beginning of the twentieth century. Images that are perceivable at a glance are the dream of advertising agencies and parallel the interest of the Minimalists in the overall gestalt of an artwork rather than the perception of individual parts.

Along with the images of Warhol and Disney, Haring's work has become one of the common visual languages of our time. During the seven weeks that the exhibition of works by Keith Haring, Andy Warhol, and Walt Disney was on view at the Phoenix Art Museum nearly 50,000 people came to see it, totalling 25 percent of our normal annual attendance. Some came to see Disney or Warhol and discovered Haring, but even those who were not familiar with Haring's work recognized it once they saw it.

Even when Haring painted in a style amalgamating Miró's, Léger's, and Calder's floating primary colors, along with Picasso's multiple perspectives and interlocking planes (as in the *Red-Yellow-Blue* series, catalogue numbers 142–45), the images retain a cartoon-like flavor. The cartooning that Haring first learned at his father's side, the cartooning that is the vehicle of his line, which is in turn the basis of his art, informs everything he made.

If cartooning informs the paintings, toys are what Haring had in mind when he started making sculpture in 1986. He had previously painted and drawn on pre-existing three-dimensional objects (catalogue numbers 120–21, 123, and 134–36), but with the sculptures, beginning in 1985, he drew in steel. Working with his typical sense of play and improvisation, Haring cut figures out of cardboard to make the models for sculptures like *Head-Stand* (catalogue number 167). Alternatively, he had plastic or wooden models built from drawings. Later, when he was more experienced, he sometimes drew with chalk–his subway drawing material– directly on the large steel plates. Rounding the edges so children could climb on them without getting hurt made the contours resemble soft chalk lines more than cut steel. Haring noted that "Painted, they no longer look like metal but like bright, shiny toys that should be played with."[22]

Pyramid (catalogue number 188) had to be withdrawn from the exhibition's tour because neither security guards nor barriers could prevent kids from climbing on it and we were afraid they would tumble onto the hard floor. Keith would have loved that children find this work so irresistible.

Steel apparently was the substance of immortality to Haring, like bronze had been to Degas. "A painting, to a degree, is still an illusion on a material," Haring said. "But once you cut this thing out of steel and put it up, it is a real thing. ... It would survive a nuclear blast probably. It has this permanent, real feeling that will exist much much much longer than I will ever exist, so it's a kind of immortality, I suppose."[23]

The Last Painting   The last painting Haring executed in his New York studio, *Untitled* (1989) (catalogue number 182), depicts a crowd of figures painted against a yellow background like that of many of his tarpaulins. The figures raise their arms in a gesture that would be a supplication except that they connect to the sides of their heads. Either the figures are hunching their shoulders in anxiety or their elbowless arms are wings and this is a host of angels.

Haring's characteristic energized line has slowed down to a crawl and the space has been filled with claustrophobic decorative marks. As they often do in the paintings, the lines run, only here they lack the optimistic, affirmative quality of Haring's earlier art. They not only run. They weep.

Keith Haring died of AIDS on February 16, 1990, at 4:40 in the morning. Born on May 4, 1958, he was thirty-one years old. In a typically generous remark in 1988 Haring said: "I think I'm just part of the circle. I think that even what I am doing is only a step in the right direction. Other people are going to take it further."[24]

Haring artistically enfranchised the lower-class black and Hispanic graffiti artists whose art he admired, acknowledged and incorporated popular art and its context into his art, and extended the fine art accomplishments of Andy Warhol into a less class-ridden realm. Taking his art out of galleries and museums, he removed it from requiring the sanctions of art critics and collectors before the public could see it, presenting it directly to his audience instead.

Haring blurred the boundaries between folk art, popular art, and fine art, genres shot through with class distinctions, racial politics, and economic implications. Other artists have attempted similar blurring, most often between popular art and fine art, and nearly always with a fine art bias. Adding folk art to the other two genres, Haring created a new territory somewhere between all three, a realm his art occupies with greater authority and conviction than anyone's. Other artists could conceivably "take it further," but so far nobody has.

151

Keith Haring with students of South Mountain High School.
Phoenix Mural, *1986, Central and Adams Street, Phoenix. Housepaint*
on plywood, 12 x 150 feet.

119   *Untitled (Mickey Mouse)*, 1981

120 *A Pair of Corinthian Columns*, 1982

121   *Untitled (Headboard),* 1982

122   *Untitled (Face with Three Eyes)*, 1982

123 *Folding Screen*, 1983

124   *Untitled (for Interview Magazine),* 1984

125   *Untitled (Free South Africa)*, 1984

126 *Andy Mouse*, 1985

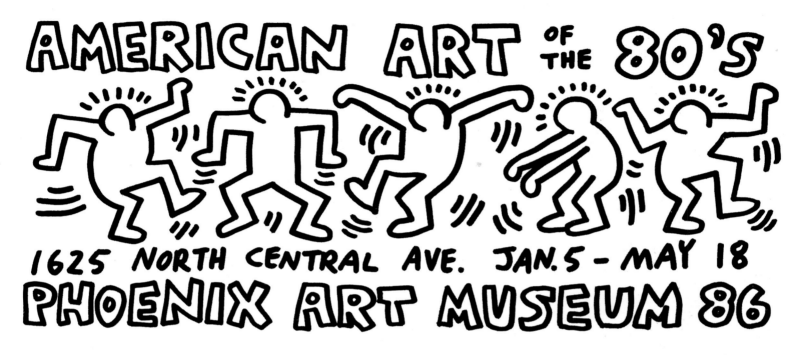

BILLBOARD DESIGN - NOV. 27- 1985 - ©K. Haring

CHILDRENS VILLAGE LOGO - SEPT. 3-85 ©K. Haring ⊕

128   *Children's Village Logo*, 1985

129   *Shoelace Design*, 1985

SHOELACE DESIGN - APRIL 11 1985 ©K. HARING ⊕ K. Haring

130   *Andy Mouse*, 1985

131 *Andy Mouse* from the portfolio *Andy Mouse,* 1986

132 *Andy Mouse* from the portfolio *Andy Mouse*, 1986

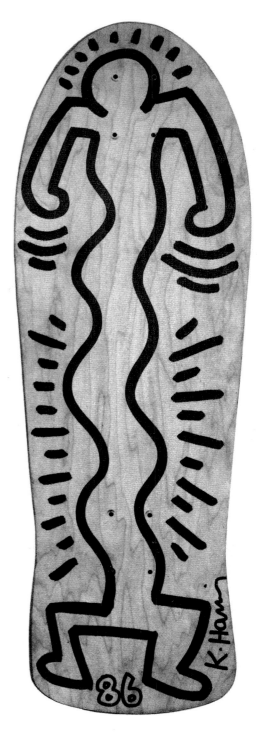

134   *Untitled (Skateboard),* 1986   135   *Untitled (Skateboard),* 1986   136   *Untitled (Skateboard),* 1986

137   *Untitled*, 1986

138 *"Birth" Images*, 1986

DRAWING FOR CTW "BE SMART" ©K. Haring 1986 July 25 MILANO

139   *Drawing for CTW "Be Smart,"* 1986

142   *Red-Yellow-Blue #10*, 1987

143   *Red-Yellow-Blue #15*, 1987

144 *Red-Yellow-Blue #23 (Portrait of Brion Gysin)*, 1987

145   *Red-Yellow-Blue #25*, 1987

146 *Knokke #10*, 1987

147   *Block Head*, 1987

148   *Cat Hat*, 1987

149   *Whassup?*, 1987

150   *Chilly Willy*, 1987

DANCY
NANCY
© K. Haring 87

151   *Dancy Nancy*, 1987

© K. Haring 87

152   *Inserts (A Very Special Christmas)*, 1987

153   *Possible Inserts*, 1987

157   *AIDS Benefit Logo*, 1987

159   *Bipo Cover*, 1987

161   *Untitled* (from a "Group of 22 Drawings"), 1987

162   *Untitled* (from a "Group of 22 Drawings"), 1987

163   *Untitled* (from a "Group of 22 Drawings"), 1987

Oct. 3 1987 © K. Haring. [A]

164   *Untitled* (from a "Group of 23 Drawings"), 1987

165   *Untitled* (from a "Group of 23 Drawings"), 1987

[A] Oct. 3 1987 © K. Haring ∅

166   *Untitled* (from a "Group of 23 Drawings"), 1987

KICK AIDS 88 WORLD TOUR

PELE AND LIZA MINELLI - CO-CHAIRS

©K.Haring POSTER DESIGN - MAY 26 1988

168   Poster Design "Kick AIDS 88", 1988

167 *Head-Stand*, 1987–88

169   *Untitled* (from "*20 Untitled Drawings*"), 1988

170   *Untitled* (from "*20 Untitled Drawings*"), 1988

171   *Pig*, 1988

173   *Dress Up Clothes*, 1988

FUNNY
BUNNY
©K·Haring 88

172   *Funny Bunny*, 1988

DRESS-UP CLOTHES © K. Haring · JAN 12 - 88

174   *Dress Up Clothes*, 1988

MATTHEW
ARTHUR
JOHANNES
OLDEN

TUESDAY MAY 3, 1988
9:18 P.M.

175   *Birth Announcement*, 1988

© K Haring JAN. 24 - 1989 ⊕

176   *Untitled (Pop Shop Billboard)*, 1989

BILLBOARD DESIGN - ©K Haring 89

5.30.89 K.Haring ⊕

178   *Self Portrait* from a *Portfolio of 8 Self-Portraits*, 1989

179 *Logo Against Family Violence*, 1989

180 *Act Up for Life*, 1989

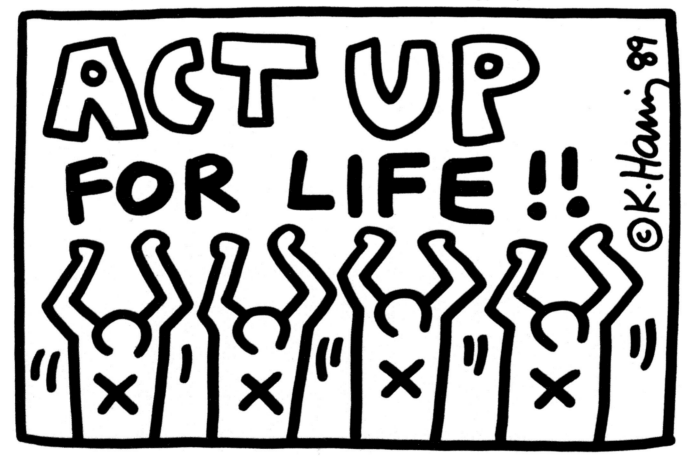

STOP AIDS
VEREINIGTE BÜHNEN WIEN
27. JUNI 1989 19.30 UHR
RAIMUNDTHEATER

181   *AIDS Poster – Vienna, 1989*

182 *Untitled*, 1989

LIL' ANGEL
©K. Haring 89

183   *Lil' Angel Design*, 1989

184   *Untitled* (*Drawing for Pyramid Sculpture*), 1990

185   *Untitled* (*Drawing for Pyramid Sculpture*), 1990

186   *Untitled* (*Drawing for Pyramid Sculpture*), 1990

187   *Untitled* (*Drawing for Pyramid Sculpture*), 1990

188 *Pyramid*, 1991

189 *Pop Shop Tokyo,* not dated

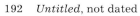

192   *Untitled*, not dated

193   *Untitled* (from "*20 Untitled Drawings*"), not dated

194   *Radiant Child* from the *Artist's Sketchbook* (*Babies, Dogs, etc.*), not dated

LIL' ANGEL
©K. Haring 89

BLOCK HEAD
K. Haring © 87

CHILLY
WILLY
K. Haring™

FUNNY
BUNNY
K. Haring™

195   *Lil' Angel, Block Head, Chilly Willi, Funny*
Bunny, Cat Hat, Whassup?, Dancy Nancy, not dated

CAT HAT
K. Haring™

WHASSUP?
© K. Haring 87

DANCY
NANCY
K. Haring™

Catalogue of the Exhibition

Walt Disney

1
Walt Disney Company
Ub Iwerks
Steamboat Willie,
animation drawing, 1 of 5, 1928
pencil on paper, 10 x 12″
Lent by Mr. & Mrs. Bruce Hamilton
© Disney

2
Walt Disney Company
Ub Iwerks
Steamboat Willie,
animation drawing, 2 of 5, 1928
pencil on paper, 10 x 12″
Lent by Mr. & Mrs. Bruce Hamilton
© Disney

3
Walt Disney Company
Ub Iwerks
Steamboat Willie,
animation drawing, 3 of 5, 1928
pencil on paper, 10 x 12″
Lent by Mr. & Mrs. Bruce Hamilton
© Disney

4
Walt Disney Company
Ub Iwerks
Steamboat Willie,
animation drawing, 4 of 5, 1928
pencil on paper, 10 x 12″
Lent by Mr. & Mrs. Bruce Hamilton
© Disney

5
Walt Disney Company
Ub Iwerks
Steamboat Willie,
animation drawing, 5 of 5, 1928
pencil on paper, 10 x 12″
Lent by Mr. & Mrs. Bruce Hamilton
© Disney

6
Walt Disney Company
Mickey Mouse – "The Mad Doctor," 1933
lithographic poster, 41 x 27″
Lent by Mr. & Mrs. Bruce Hamilton
© Disney

7
Walt Disney Company
Silly Symphonies "The Wise Little Hen,"
1934
pen and ink and gray wash on
animation paper, 8 x 12¾″
Lent by Mr. & Mrs. Bruce Hamilton
© Disney

8
Walt Disney Company
Ferdinand Horvath
"Snow White in the Evil Forest" from
Snow White and the Seven Dwarfs, c. 1936
pencil on paper, 7½ x 11¼″
Lent by Mr. & Mrs. Bruce Hamilton
© Disney

9
Walt Disney Company
Little Hiawatha,
Courvoisier cel set-up, 1937
pigment on board and celluloid, 6¼ x 4¾″
Phoenix Art Museum Collection, 00.58.6
© Disney

10
Walt Disney Company
Little Hiawatha (with his pants down),
Courvoisier cel set-up, 1937
pigment on board and celluloid, 7¼ x 6½″
Phoenix Art Museum Collection, 00.58.7
© Disney

11
Walt Disney Company
Silly Symphonies "Little Hiawatha," 1937
silkscreen poster, 60 x 40″
Lent by Mr. & Mrs. Bruce Hamilton
© Disney

12
Walt Disney Company
Mickey Mouse "Magician Mickey," 1937
silkscreen poster, 60 x 40″
Lent by Mr. & Mrs. Bruce Hamilton
© Disney

13
Walt Disney Company
Gustaf Tenggren
Pinocchio
(original concept of the opening scene),
c. 1937; watercolor on paper, 10¾ x 15¾″
Lent by Mr. & Mrs. Bruce Hamilton
© Disney

14
Walt Disney Company
"Snow White (with Rabbits)" from *Snow
White and the Seven Dwarfs,*
Courvoisier cel set-up, 1937
pigment on board and celluloid, 8¼ x 7⅞″
Phoenix Art Museum Collection, 00.58.9
© Disney

15
Walt Disney Company
"Snow White (at a window)" from *Snow
White and the Seven Dwarfs,*
Courvoisier cel set-up, 1937
pigment on board and celluloid, 7½ x 8⅝″
Phoenix Art Museum Collection, 00.58.10
© Disney

16
Walt Disney Company
"Snow White (with the Prince in the
Forest)" from *Snow White and the
+Seven Dwarfs,*
production cel set-up, 1937
pigment on board and celluloid, 7 x 14″
Phoenix Art Museum Collection, 00.58.2
© Disney

17
Walt Disney Company
Brave Little Tailor,
Courvoisier cel set-up, 1938
original animation by Les Clark
pigment on board and celluloid, 7¼ x 6¼″
Phoenix Art Museum Collection, 00.58.9
© Disney

18
Walt Disney Company
Les Clark
Brave Little Tailor,
clean-up animation extreme, 1 of 9, 1938
graphite and colored pencil on paper,
10 x 12″
Lent by the Walt Disney Company
© Disney

19
Walt Disney Company
Les Clark
Brave Little Tailor,
clean-up animation extreme, 2 of 9, 1938
graphite and colored pencil on paper,
10 x 12″
Lent by the Walt Disney Company
© Disney

20
Walt Disney Company
Les Clark
Brave Little Tailor,
clean-up animation extreme, 3 of 9, 1938
graphite and colored pencil on paper,
10 x 12″
Lent by the Walt Disney Company
© Disney

21
Walt Disney Company
Les Clark
Brave Little Tailor,
clean-up animation extreme, 4 of 9, 1938
graphite and colored pencil on paper,
10 x 12″
Lent by the Walt Disney Company
© Disney

22
Walt Disney Company
Les Clark
Brave Little Tailor,
clean-up animation extreme, 5 of 9, 1938
graphite and colored pencil on paper,
10 x 12″
Lent by the Walt Disney Company
© Disney

23
Walt Disney Company
Les Clark
Brave Little Tailor,
clean-up animation extreme, 6 of 9, 1938
graphite and colored pencil on paper,
10 x 12″
Lent by the Walt Disney Company
© Disney

24
Walt Disney Company
Les Clark
Brave Little Tailor,
clean-up animation extreme, 7 of 9, 1938
graphite and colored pencil on paper,
10 x 12″
Lent by the Walt Disney Company
© Disney

25
Walt Disney Company
Les Clark
Brave Little Tailor,
clean-up animation extreme, 8 of 9, 1938
graphite and colored pencil on paper,
10 x 12″
Lent by the Walt Disney Company
© Disney

26
Walt Disney Company
Les Clark
Brave Little Tailor,
clean-up animation extreme, 9 of 9, 1938
graphite and colored pencil on paper,
10 x 12″
Lent by the Walt Disney Company
© Disney

27
Walt Disney Company
Brave Little Tailor, cel set-up, 1938
pigment on board and celluloid, 9 x 10½″
Lent by George F. Getz, Jr.
© Disney

28
Walt Disney Company
Brave Little Tailor, cel set-up, 1938
pigment on board and celluloid, 8¾ x 11½″
Lent by George F. Getz, Jr.
© Disney

29
Walt Disney Company
Brave Little Tailor, cel set-up, 1938
pigment on board and celluloid, 8¼ x 8¾″
Lent by George F. Getz, Jr.
© Disney

30
Walt Disney Company
Brave Little Tailor, cel set-up, 1938
pigment on board and celluloid, 8¾ x 11¼″
Lent by George F. Getz, Jr.
© Disney

31
Walt Disney Company
Brave Little Tailor, cel set-up, 1938
pigment on board and celluloid, 9 x 12¼″
Lent by George F. Getz, Jr.
© Disney

32
Walt Disney Company
Brave Little Tailor, cel set-up, 1938
pigment on board and celluloid, 9¼ x 7″
Lent by George F. Getz, Jr.
© Disney

33
Walt Disney Company
Brave Little Tailor, cel set-up, 1938
pigment on board and celluloid, 8 x 8¾″
Lent by George F. Getz, Jr.
© Disney

34
Walt Disney Company
Society Dog Show, cel set-up, 1938
pigment on board and celluloid, 8 x 9½″
Lent by George F. Getz, Jr.
© Disney

35
Walt Disney Company
Howard Swift
"Ferdinand and Matador" from
Ferdinand the Bull,
Courvoisier cel set-up, 1938
original animation by: Milt Kahl for
Ferdinand; Ward Kimball for the Matador
pigment on board an celluloid, 9 x 9¼″
Phoenix Art Museum Collection, 00.58.1
© Disney

36
Disney Company
Ward Kimball
Ferdinand the Bull, clean-up animation
extreme, 1 of 6, 1938
graphite and colored pencil on paper,
10 x 12″
Lent by the Walt Disney Company
© Disney

37
Walt Disney Company
Ward Kimball
Ferdinand the Bull, clean-up animation
extreme, 2 of 6, 1938
graphite and colored pencil on paper,
10 x 12″
Lent by the Walt Disney Company
© Disney

38
Walt Disney Company
Ward Kimball
Ferdinand the Bull, clean-up animation
extreme, 3 of 6, 1938
graphite and colored pencil on paper,
10 x 12″
Lent by the Walt Disney Company
© Disney

39
Walt Disney Company
Ward Kimball
Ferdinand the Bull, clean-up animation
extreme, 4 of 6, 1938
graphite and colored pencil on paper,
10 x 12″
Lent by the Walt Disney Company
© Disney

40
Walt Disney Company
Ward Kimball
Ferdinand the Bull, clean-up animation
extreme, 5 of 6, 1938
graphite and colored pencil on paper,
10 x 12″
Lent by the Walt Disney Company
© Disney

41
Walt Disney Company
Ward Kimball
Ferdinand the Bull, clean-up animation
extreme, 6 of 6, 1938
graphite and colored pencil on paper,
10 x 12″
Lent by the Walt Disney Company
© Disney

42
Walt Disney Company
The Pointer, cel set-up, 1939
pigment on board and celluloid, 8¼ x 11″
Lent by George F. Getz, Jr.
© Disney

43
Walt Disney Company
The Pointer, 1939
serigraph on celluloid, 10 x 14″
Lent by George F. Getz, Jr.
© Disney

44
Walt Disney Company
The Pointer, cel set-up, 1939
pigment on board and celluloid, 8¼ x 10¾″
Lent by George F. Getz, Jr.
© Disney

45
Walt Disney Company
Silly Symphonies "The Practical Pig,"
1939
lithographic poster, 41 x 27″
Lent by Mr. & Mrs. Bruce Hamilton
© Disney

46
Walt Disney Company
Donald Duck "Beach Picnic," 1939
pen and ink drawing of the poster,
12 x 8¾″
Lent by Mr. & Mrs. Bruce Hamilton
© Disney

47
Walt Disney Company
Donald Duck "Beach Picnic," 1939
lithographic poster, 41 x 27″
Lent by Mr. & Mrs. Bruce Hamilton
© Disney

48
Walt Disney Company
The Ugly Duckling, Courvoisier cel
set-up, 1939
pigment on board and celluloid,
5⁵⁄₁₆ x 7³⁄₁₆″
Phoenix Art Museum Collection, 00.58.11
© Disney

49
Walt Disney Company
The Practical Pig, Courvoisier cel set-up,
1939
pigment on board and celluloid, 8⅛ x 10½″
Phoenix Art Museum Collection, 00.58.13
© Disney

50
Walt Disney Company
Donald's Cousin Gus, 1939
pen and ink drawing of the poster,
12 x 8¾″
Lent by Mr. & Mrs. Bruce Hamilton
© Disney

51
Walt Disney Company
Donald's Cousin Gus, 1939
lithographic poster, 41 x 27″
Lent by Mr. & Mrs. Bruce Hamilton
© Disney

52
Walt Disney Company
*Donald's Penguin, "Donald Duck and
Tootsie,"*
Courvoisier cel set-up, 1939
pigment on board and celluloid, 8½ x 9¾″
Phoenix Art Museum Collection, 00.58.14
© Disney

53
Walt Disney Company
Fantasia, cel set-up, 1940
pigment on board and celluloid, 7¾ x 10″
Lent by George F. Getz, Jr.
© Disney

54
Walt Disney Company
Howard Swift
Fantasia, "Dance of the Hours,"
animation extreme, 1 of 6, 1940
graphite and colored pencil on paper,
10 x 12″
Lent by the Walt Disney Company
© Disney

55
Walt Disney Company
Howard Swift
Fantasia, "Dance of the Hours,"
animation extreme, 2 of 6, 1940
graphite and colored pencil on paper,
10 x 12″
Lent by the Walt Disney Company
© Disney

56
Walt Disney Company
Howard Swift
Fantasia, "Dance of the Hours,"
animation extreme, 3 of 6, 1940
graphite and colored pencil on paper,
10 x 12″
Lent by the Walt Disney Company
© Disney

57
Walt Disney Company
Howard Swift
Fantasia, "Dance of the Hours,"
animation extreme, 4 of 6, 1940
graphite and colored pencil on paper,
10 x 12″
Lent by the Walt Disney Company
© Disney

58
Walt Disney Company
Howard Swift
Fantasia, "Dance of the Hours,"
animation extreme, 5 of 6, 1940
graphite and colored pencil on paper,
10 x 12″
Lent by the Walt Disney Company
© Disney

59
Walt Disney Company
Howard Swift
Fantasia, "Dance of the Hours,"
animation extreme, 6 of 6, 1940
graphite and colored pencil on paper,
10 x 12″
Lent by the Walt Disney Company
© Disney

60
Walt Disney Company
Fantasia, "Dance of the Hours,"
Courvoisier cel set-up, 1940
original animation by Howard Swift
pigment on board and celluloid, 9 x 8″
Phoenix Art Museum Collection, 00.58.12
© Disney

61
Walt Disney Company
Jiminey, from *"Pinocchio,"* Courvoisier
cel set-up, 1940
pigment on board and celluloid, 5¾ x 4¾″
Phoenix Art Museum Collection, 00.58.4
© Disney

62
Walt Disney Company
Jiminey, from *"Pinocchio,"* Courvoisier
cel set-up, 1940
pigment on board and celluloid, 5¾ x 4¾″,
image size
Phoenix Art Museum Collection, 00.58.3
© Disney

63
Walt Disney Company
Cleo, from *"Pinocchio,"* Courvoisier cel
set-up, 1940
pigment on board and celluoid, 5¹¹⁄₁₆ x 6½″
Phoenix Art Museum Collection, 00.58.9
© Disney

64
Walt Disney Company
Mickey with a Lasso, not dated
graphite on paper, 8 x 5½″
Lent by George F. Getz, Jr.
© Disney

65
Walt Disney Company
Minnie and Mickey Mouse at a Piano,
not dated
lithograph, ink and watercolor, 8¾ x 6½″
Lent by George F. Getz, Jr.
© Disney

66
Walt Disney Company
Snow White, c. 1953
lithographic poster, 81½ x 41″
Lent by Mr. & Mrs. Bruce Hamilton
© Disney

67
Walt Disney Company
Carl Barks
Halloween in Duckburg, 1973
oil on board, 18 x 24″
Lent by Mr. and Mrs. Kerby Confer
© Disney

68
Walt Disney Company
Vance Gerry
The Prince and the Pauper,
story sketch, 1990
grease pencil on paper, 5½ x 8½″
Lent by the Walt Disney Company
© Disney

69
Walt Disney Company
Andreas Deja
The Prince and the Pauper,
rough animation, 1 of 4, 1990
pencil on paper, 12½ x 17″
Lent by the Walt Disney Company
© Disney

70
Walt Disney Company
Andreas Deja
The Prince and the Pauper,
rough animation, 2 of 4, 1990
pencil on paper, 12½ x 17″
Lent by the Walt Disney Company
© Disney

71
Walt Disney Company
Andreas Deja
The Prince and the Pauper,
rough animation, 3 of 4, 1990
pencil on paper, 12½ x 17″
Lent by the Walt Disney Company
© Disney

72
Walt Disney Company
Andreas Deja
The Prince and the Pauper,
rough animation, 4 of 4, 1990
pencil on paper, 12½ x 17″
Lent by the Walt Disney Company
© Disney

73
Walt Disney Company
Kathy Bailey
The Prince and the Pauper,
clean-up animation, 1 of 4, 1990
pencil on paper, 12½ x 17″
Lent by the Walt Disney Company
© Disney

74
Walt Disney Company
Kathy Bailey
The Prince and the Pauper,
clean-up animation, 2 of 4, 1990
pencil on paper, 12½ x 17″
Lent by the Walt Disney Company
© Disney

75
Walt Disney Company
Kathy Bailey
The Prince and the Pauper, clean-up
animation, 3 of 4, 1990
pencil on paper, 12½ x 17″
Lent by the Walt Disney Company
© Disney

76
Walt Disney Company
Kathy Bailey
The Prince and the Pauper, clean-up
animation, 4 of 4, 1990
pencil on paper, 12½ 2 x 17″
Lent by the Walt Disney Company
© Disney

77
Walt Disney Company
The Prince and the Pauper, cel
set-up, 1990
Background painting by Greg Drolette
gouache on paper, 13½ x 43¾″
Lent by the Walt Disney Company
© Disney

Andy Warhol

78
Andy Warhol
*The Men in Her Life (Mike Todd and
Eddie Fisher),* 1962 & 1978
synthetic polymer silkscreened on canvas,
12⅞ x 80″
Lent by Margo Leavin Gallery,
Los Angeles
© The Andy Warhol Foundation for the
Visual Arts, Inc., New York

79
Andy Warhol
Warren, 1962
acrylic and silkscreen on canvas,
13⅞ x 10″
Lent by The Andy Warhol Foundation for
the Visual Arts, Inc., New York
© The Andy Warhol Foundation for the
Visual Arts, Inc., New York

80
Andy Warhol
Troy, 1962-63
acrylic and silkscreen on canvas,
13⅞ x 10″
Lent by The Andy Warhol Foundation for
the Visual Arts, Inc., New York
© The Andy Warhol Foundation for the
Visual Arts, Inc., New York

81
Andy Warhol
Andy Warhol, 1963
photobooth pictures, strip of four images,
7¾ x 1½″
Lent by Robert Miller Gallery, Inc.,
New York
© The Andy Warhol Foundation for the
Visual Arts, Inc., New York

82
Andy Warhol
Ethel Scull, 1963
photobooth pictures, strip of four images,
7¾ x 1½″
Lent by Robert Miller Gallery, Inc.,
New York
© The Andy Warhol Foundation for the
Visual Arts, Inc., New York

83
** Andy Warhol
Jacqueline Kennedy, 1964
silkscreen on canvas, 20 x 128″
Lent by The Robert B. Mayer Memorial
Loan Collection
© The Andy Warhol Foundation for the
Visual Arts, Inc., New York

84
Andy Warhol
Taylor Mead, c. 1966
photobooth pictures, strip of four images,
7¾ x 1½"
Lent by Robert Miller Gallery, Inc.,
New York
© The Andy Warhol Foundation for the
Visual Arts, Inc., New York

85
Andy Warhol
Edie Sedgwick, c. 1966
photobooth pictures, strip of four images,
7¾ x 1½"
Lent by Robert Miller Gallery, Inc.,
New York
© The Andy Warhol Foundation for the
Visual Arts, Inc., New York

86
Andy Warhol
Unidentified (Jackson Browne?), c. 1966
photobooth pictures, strip of four images,
7¾ x 1½"
Lent by Robert Miller Gallery, Inc.,
New York
© The Andy Warhol Foundation for the
Visual Arts, Inc., New York

87
* Andy Warhol
Marilyn, 1967
portfolio of 10 screenprints, 36 x 36" each
Lent by the Frederick R. Weisman Art
Foundation, Los Angeles
© The Andy Warhol Foundation for the
Visual Arts, Inc., New York

88
* Andy Warhol
Self-Portrait, 1967
silkscreen enamel on synthetic polymer
paint on canvas, 72 x 72"
Lent by Mr. and Mrs. Harry W. Anderson
© The Andy Warhol Foundation for the
Visual Arts, Inc., New York

89
** Andy Warhol
Untitled (Campbell's Soup Can), 1967
graphite on paper, 17 x 14"
Lent by the University Art Museum,
University of New Mexico,
purchased through a grant from the
National Endowment for the Arts and the
Friends of Art
© The Andy Warhol Foundation for the
Visual Arts, Inc., New York

90
Andy Warhol
Sandra Brant, 1968
photobooth pictures, strip of four images,
7¾ x 1½"
Lent by Robert Miller Gallery, Inc.,
New York
© The Andy Warhol Foundation for the
Visual Arts, Inc., New York

91
Andy Warhol
Kellogg's Boxes (Corn Flakes), 1971
silkscreen ink on wood
24 boxes, 27 x 24 x 19" each
Lent by the Los Angeles County Museum
of Art, gift of Andy Warhol through the
Contemporary Art Council Fund
© The Andy Warhol Foundation for the
Visual Arts, Inc., New York

92
Andy Warhol
Mao Tse-Tung, 1972
screenprint from the portfolio of 10,
36 x 36"
Lent by Martin Lawrence Limited
Editions, Van Nuys, California
© The Andy Warhol Foundation for the
Visual Arts, Inc., New York

93
Andy Warhol
Mao Tse-Tung, 1972
screenprint from the portfolio of 10,
36 x 36"
Lent by Martin Lawrence Limited
Editions, Van Nuys, California
© The Andy Warhol Foundation for the
Visual Arts, Inc., New York

94
Andy Warhol
Mao Tse-Tung, 1972
screenprint from the portfolio of 10,
36 x 36"
Lent by Martin Lawrence Limited
Editions, Van Nuys, California
© The Andy Warhol Foundation for the
Visual Arts, Inc., New York

95
Andy Warhol
Brooke Shields, 1976-86
stitched gelatin silver prints, 22 x 28"
Lent by Mr. and Mrs. William H. Bonifas
© The Andy Warhol Foundation for the
Visual Arts, Inc., New York

96
Andy Warhol
The Marx Brothers from the portfolio *Ten
Portraits of Jews of the Twentieth
Century,* 1980
screenprint, 40 x 32"
Lent by Ronald Feldman Fine Arts,
New York
© The Andy Warhol Foundation for the
Visual Arts, Inc., New York, and Ronald
Feldman Fine Arts, New York

97
Andy Warhol
Joseph Beuys, State III, 1980/83
screenprint, 40 x 32"
Lent by Editions Schellman, Munich-
New York
© The Andy Warhol Foundation for the
Visual Arts, Inc., New York

98
* Andy Warhol
Myths: Mickey Mouse, 1981
magic marker on paper, 12¼ x 15⅞"
Lent by The Andy Warhol Foundation for
the Visual Arts, Inc., New York
© The Andy Warhol Foundation for the
Visual Arts, Inc., New York

99
Andy Warhol
The Star (Garbo) from the portfolio
Myths, 1981
screenprint, 38 x 38"
Lent by Ronald Feldman Fine Arts,
New York
© The Andy Warhol Foundation for the
Visual Arts, Inc., New York, and Ronald
Feldman Fine Arts, New York

100
Andy Warhol
Uncle Sam from the portfolio *Myths,* 1981
screenprint, 38 x 38"
Lent by Ronald Feldman Fine Arts,
New York
© The Andy Warhol Foundation for the
Visual Arts, Inc., New York, and Ronald
Feldman Fine Arts, New York

101
Andy Warhol
Superman from the portfolio *Myths,* 1981
screenprint, 38 x 38"
Lent by Ronald Feldman Fine Arts,
New York
© The Andy Warhol Foundation for the
Visual Arts, Inc., New York, and Ronald
Feldman Fine Arts, New York

102
Andy Warhol
The Witch from the portfolio *Myths,* 1981
screenprint, 38 x 38"
Lent by Ronald Feldman Fine Arts,
New York
© The Andy Warhol Foundation for the
Visual Arts, Inc., New York, and Ronald
Feldman Fine Arts, New York

103
Andy Warhol
Mammy from the portfolio *Myths,* 1981
screenprint, 38 x 38"
Lent by Ronald Feldman Fine Arts,
New York
© The Andy Warhol Foundation for the
Visual Arts, Inc., New York, and Ronald
Feldman Fine Arts, New York

104
Andy Warhol
Howdy Doody from the portfolio *Myths,*
1981
screenprint, 38 x 38″
Lent by Ronald Feldman Fine Arts,
New York
© The Andy Warhol Foundation for the
Visual Arts, Inc., New York, and Ronald
Feldman Fine Arts, New York

105
Andy Warhol
Dracula from the portfolio *Myths,* 1981
screenprint, 38 x 38″
Lent by Ronald Feldman Fine Arts,
New York
© The Andy Warhol Foundation for the
Visual Arts, Inc., New York, and Ronald
Feldman Fine Arts, New York

106
Andy Warhol
Mickey Mouse from the portfolio *Myths,*
1981
screenprint, 38 x 38″
Lent by Ronald Feldman Fine Arts,
New York
© The Andy Warhol Foundation for the
Visual Arts, Inc., New York, and Ronald
Feldman Fine Arts, New York

107
Andy Warhol
Santa Claus from the portfolio *Myths,*
1981
screenprint, 38 x 38″
Lent by Ronald Feldman Fine Arts,
New York
© The Andy Warhol Foundation for the
Visual Arts, Inc., New York, and Ronald
Feldman Fine Arts, New York

108
Andy Warhol
The Shadow from the portfolio *Myths,*
1981
screenprint, 38 x 38″
Lent by Ronald Feldman Fine Arts,
New York
© The Andy Warhol Foundation for the
Visual Arts, Inc., New York, and Ronald
Feldman Fine Arts, New York

109
Andy Warhol
*Portrait of Keith Haring and Juan
Dubose,* 1983
synthetic polymer silkscreened on canvas,
40 x 40″
Lent by The Estate of Keith Haring
© The Andy Warhol Foundation for the
Visual Arts, Inc., New York

110
Andy Warhol
*Portrait of Keith Haring and Juan
Dubose,* 1984
synthetic polymer silkscreened on canvas,
40 x 40″
Lent by The Estate of Keith Haring
© The Andy Warhol Foundation for the
Visual Arts, Inc., New York

111
Andy Warhol
Grace Kelly, 1984
screenprint, 40 x 32″
Lent by Ronald Feldman Fine Arts,
New York
© The Andy Warhol Foundation for the
Visual Arts, Inc., New York, and Ronald
Feldman Fine Arts, New York

112
Andy Warhol
Blackglama (Judy Garland) from the
portfolio *Ads,* 1985
screenprint, 38 x 38″ each
Lent by Ronald Feldman Fine Arts,
New York
© The Andy Warhol Foundation for the
Visual Arts, Inc., New York, and Ronald
Feldman Fine Arts, New York

113
Andy Warhol
Rebel Without a Cause (James Dean) from
the portfolio *Ads,* 1985
screenprint, 38 x 38″
Lent by Ronald Feldman Fine Arts,
New York
© The Andy Warhol Foundation for the
Visual Arts, Inc., New York, and Ronald
Feldman Fine Arts, New York

114
Andy Warhol
Van Heusen (Ronald Reagan) from the
portfolio *Ads,* 1985
screenprint, 38 x 38″
Lent by Ronald Feldman Fine Arts,
New York
© The Andy Warhol Foundation for the
Visual Arts, Inc., New York, and Ronald
Feldman Fine Arts, New York

115
Andy Warhol
The New Spirit (Donald Duck) from the
portfolio *Ads,* 1985
screenprint, 38 x 38″
Lent by Ronald Feldman Fine Arts,
New York
© The Andy Warhol Foundation for the
Visual Arts, Inc., New York, and Ronald
Feldman Fine Arts, New York

116
Andy Warhol
Anniversary Donald Duck, 1985
screenprint, 30½ x 43″
Lent by Ronald Feldman Fine Arts,
New York
© The Andy Warhol Foundation for the
Visual Arts, Inc., New York, and Ronald
Feldman Fine Arts, New York

117
**Andy Warhol
Dolly Parton, 1985
silkscreen ink on synthetic polymer paint
on canvas, 42 x 42″
Lent by The Andy Warhol Foundation for
the Visual Arts, Inc., New York
© The Andy Warhol Foundation for the
Visual Arts, Inc., New York

118
**Andy Warhol
Dolly Parton, 1985
silkscreen ink on synthetic polymer paint
on canvas, 42 x 42″
Lent by The Andy Warhol Foundation for
the Visual Arts, Inc., New York
© The Andy Warhol Foundation for the
Visual Arts, Inc., New York

Keith Haring

119
Keith Haring
Untitled (Mickey Mouse), 1981
black ink on paper, 38¼ x 50″
Lent by The Estate of Keith Haring,
KHD 852
© The Estate of Keith Haring, New York

120
Keith Haring with L.A. II (Angel Ortiz)
A Pair of Corinthian Columns, 1982
dayglo and black ink on fiberglass
columns, 118 x 20 x 20″
Lent by The Estate of Keith Haring, KHS
111/1, 111/2
© The Estate of Keith Haring, New York

121
Keith Haring
Untitled (Headboard), 1982
dayglo, enamel and black felt-tip pen on
metal headboard, 56 x 54⅝ x 4¼″
Lent by The Estate of Keith Haring,
KHS 23
© The Estate of Keith Haring, New York

122
Keith Haring
Untitled (Face with Three Eyes), 1982
dayglo on board, 20½ x 24 x ¾″
Lent by The Estate of Keith Haring,
KHS 38
© The Estate of Keith Haring, New York

123
Keith Haring
Folding Screen, 1983
gouache and blue ink on yellow paper,
36 x 65″
Lent by The Estate of Keith Haring,
KHS 78
© The Estate of Keith Haring, New York

124
Keith Haring
Untitled (for Interview magazine), 1984
black ink on paper, 36 x 24″
Lent by The Estate of Keith Haring,
KHD 85
© The Estate of Keith Haring, New York

125
Keith Haring
Untitled (Free South Africa), 1984
black ink and gouache on paper,
32¼ x 40⅛″
Lent by The Estate of Keith Haring,
KHD 358
© The Estate of Keith Haring, New York

126
Keith Haring
Andy Mouse, 1985
acrylic on canvas, 60 x 60″
Lent by The Estate of Keith Haring,
KHC 16
© The Estate of Keith Haring, New York

127
Keith Haring
American Art of the 1980s, 1985
black felt-tip pen on paper, 7¼ x 14″
Lent by The Estate of Keith Haring,
926/23, 3/23
© The Estate of Keith Haring, New York

128
Keith Haring
Children's Village Logo, 1985
black felt-tip pen on paper, 11 x 14″
Lent by The Estate of Keith Haring, KHD
929/38, 28/38
© The Estate of Keith Haring, New York

129
Keith Haring
Shoelace Design, 1985
black felt-tip pen on paper, 2⅝ x 11⅞″
Lent by The Estate of Keith Haring, KHD
930/9, 7/9
© The Estate of Keith Haring, New York

130
Keith Haring
Andy Mouse, 1985
black ink on paper, 23 x 23″
Lent by The Estate of Keith Haring,
KHD 125
© The Estate of Keith Haring, New York

131
Keith Haring
Andy Mouse from the portfolio *Andy
Mouse*, 1986
screenprint, 38 x 38″
Lent by The Security Pacific Corporation
© The Estate of Keith Haring, New York

132
Keith Haring
Andy Mouse from the portfolio *Andy
Mouse*, 1986
screenprint, 38 x 38″
Lent by The Security Pacific Corporation
© The Estate of Keith Haring, New York

133
Keith Haring
Money Magazine "Andy Mouse Bill,"
1986
black felt-tip pen on paper, 11 x 14″
Lent by The Estate of Keith Haring,
KHD 790
© The Estate of Keith Haring, New York

134
Keith Haring
Untitled (Skateboard), 1986
black enamel and silver felt-tip pen on
wood, 30½ x 10¾ x ¼″
Lent by The Estate of Keith Haring,
KHS 25
© The Estate of Keith Haring, New York

135
Keith Haring
Untitled (Skateboard), 1986
black felt-tip pen on wood, 29⅞ x 9¾ x ¼″
Lent by The Estate of Keith Haring,
KHS 26
© The Estate of Keith Haring, New York

136
Keith Haring
Untitled (Skateboard), 1986
black felt-tip pen on wood, 29⅞ x 9⅞ x ¼″
Lent by The Estate of Keith Haring,
KHS 27
© The Estate of Keith Haring, New York

137
Keith Haring
Untitled, 1986
acrylic on canvas, 72¾ x 74¼″
Lent by The Estate of Keith Haring,
KHC 14
© The Estate of Keith Haring, New York

138
Keith Haring
"Birth" Images, 1986
black felt-tip pen on paper, 14 x 11″
Lent by The Estate of Keith Haring,
KHD 828
© The Estate of Keith Haring, New York

139
Keith Haring
Drawing for CTW "Be Smart," 1986
black felt-tip pen and white paint on
paper, 13¼ x 13¾″
Lent by The Estate of Keith Haring,
KHD 645
© The Estate of Keith Haring, New York

140
Keith Haring
Andy Mouse, 1986
black felt-tip pen on paper, 11 x 8½″
Lent by Martin and Janet Blinder,
Los Angeles, California
© The Estate of Keith Haring, New York

141
Keith Haring
Absolutly, 1986
acrylic and silver paint on canvas, 84 x 60″
Lent by The Estate of Keith Haring,
KHC 29
© The Estate of Keith Haring, New York

142
Keith Haring
Red-Yellow-Blue #10, 1987
acrylic and enamel on canvas, 84 x 48"
Lent by The Estate of Keith Haring,
KHC 31
© The Estate of Keith Haring, New York

143
Keith Haring
Red-Yellow-Blue #15, 1987
acrylic and enamel on canvas, 84 x 48"
Lent by The Estate of Keith Haring,
KHC 30
© The Estate of Keith Haring, New York

144
Keith Haring
Red-Yellow-Blue #23 (Portrait of Brion
Gysin), 1987
acrylic and enamel on canvas, 36 x 36"
Lent by The Estate of Keith Haring,
KHC 38
© The Estate of Keith Haring, New York

145
Keith Haring
Red-Yellow-Blue #25, 1987
acrylic and enamel on canvas, 36 x 48"
Lent by The Estate of Keith Haring,
KHC 24
© The Estate of Keith Haring, New York

146
Keith Haring
Knokke #10, 1987
acrylic and enamel on linen, 70¾ x 70¾"
Lent by The Estate of Keith Haring,
KHC 35
© The Estate of Keith Haring, New York

147
Keith Haring
Block Head, 1987
black felt-tip pen on paper, 12 x 9"
Lent by The Estate of Keith Haring,
KHD 769
© The Estate of Keith Haring, New York

148
Keith Haring
Cat Hat, 1987
black felt-tip pen on paper, 12 x 9"
Lent by The Estate of Keith Haring,
KHD 772
© The Estate of Keith Haring, New York

149
Keith Haring
Whassup?, 1987
black felt-tip on paper, 12 x 9"
Lent by The Estate of Keith Haring,
KHD 770
© The Estate of Keith Haring, New York

150
Keith Haring
Chilly Willy, 1987
black felt-tip pen on paper, 12 x 9"
Lent by The Estate of Keith Haring,
KHD 771
© The Estate of Keith Haring, New York

151
Keith Haring
Dancy Nancy, 1987
black felt-tip pen on paper, 12 x 9"
Lent by The Estate of Keith Haring,
KHD 773
© The Estate of Keith Haring, New York

152
Keith Haring
Inserts (A Very Special Christmas), 1987
black felt-tip pen on paper, 13⅞ x 16⅞"
Lent by The Estate of Keith Haring,
KHD 660
© The Estate of Keith Haring, New York

153
Keith Haring
Possible Inserts, 1987
black felt-tip pen on paper, 13⅞ x 16⅞"
Lent by The Estate of Keith Haring,
KHD 635
© The Estate of Keith Haring, New York

154
Keith Haring
*Billboard Design for the Broward County
Humane Society, Florida,* 1987
black felt-tip pen on paper, 6¾ x 15"
Lent by The Estate of Keith Haring,
KHD 712
© The Estate of Keith Haring, New York

155
Keith Haring
*Billboard for the Broward County
Humane Society, Florida,* 1987
silkscreen on paper mounted on board,
10'7" x 22'10"
Lent by The Estate of Keith Haring
© The Estate of Keith Haring, New York

156
Keith Haring
AIDS Benefit Logo, 1987
black felt-tip pen on paper, 11 x 14"
Lent by The Estate of Keith Haring,
KHD 718
© The Estate of Keith Haring, New York

157
Keith Haring
AIDS Benefit Logo, 1987
offset lithograph, crack & peel sticker,
5½ x 4⅝"
Lent by The Estate of Keith Haring
© The Estate of Keith Haring, New York

158
Keith Haring
*Channel 13 – Art Festival "Draw Me a
Story,"* 1987
black felt-tip pen on paper, 16⅞ x 14"
Lent by The Estate of Keith Haring,
KHD 643
© The Estate of Keith Haring, New York

159
Keith Haring
Bipo Cover, 1987
black felt-tip pen on paper, 14 x 16⅞"
Lent by The Estate of Keith Haring,
KHD 642
© The Estate of Keith Haring, New York

160
Keith Haring
Bipo Cover, 1987
offset lithograph, 12¼ x 12¼"
Lent by The Estate of Keith Haring
© The Estate of Keith Haring, New York

161
Keith Haring
Untitled (from a "Group of 22
Drawings"), 1987
black felt-tip pen on paper, 11⅝ x 15⅜"
Lent by The Estate of Keith Haring,
KHD 316/22, 10/22
© The Estate of Keith Haring, New York

162
Keith Haring
Untitled (from a "Group of 22
Drawings"), 1987
black felt-tip pen on paper, 11⅝ x 15⅜"
Lent by The Estate of Keith Haring,
KHD 316/22, 17/22
© The Estate of Keith Haring, New York

163
Keith Haring
Untitled (from a "Group of 22
Drawings"), 1987
black felt-tip pen on paper, 11⅝ x 15⅜"
Lent by The Estate of Keith Haring,
KHD 316/22, 21/22
© The Estate of Keith Haring, New York

164
Keith Haring
Untitled (from a "Group of 23
Drawings"), 1987
black felt-tip pen on paper, 11⅝ x 15⅜"
Lent by The Estate of Keith Haring,
KHD 317/23, 10/23
© The Estate of Keith Haring, New York

165
Keith Haring
Untitled (from a "Group of 23
Drawings"), 1987
black felt-tip pen on paper. 11⅝ x 15⅜"
Lent by The Estate of Keith Haring,
KHD 317/23, 17/23
© The Estate of Keith Haring, New York

166
Keith Haring
Untitled (from a "Group of 23
Drawings"), 1987
black felt-tip pen on paper. 11⅝ x 15⅜"
Lent by The Estate of Keith Haring,
KHD 317/23, 21/23
© The Estate of Keith Haring, New York

167
Keith Haring
Head-Stand, 1987-88
painted steel, 80¹³/₁₆ x 36⅝ x ¹¹/₁₆",
base: 45¹¹/₁₆"
Lent by Martin and Janet Blinder,
Los Angeles, California
© The Estate of Keith Haring, New York

168
Keith Haring
Poster Design "Kick AIDS 88," 1988
black ink and felt-tip pen on paper,
16⅞ x 14"
Lent by The Estate of Keith Haring,
KHD 651
© The Estate of Keith Haring, New York

169
Keith Haring
Untitled (from "*20 Untitled
Drawings*"), 1988
black ink on paper, 11 x 14"
Lent by The Estate of Keith Haring,
KHD 604/20, 12/20
© The Estate of Keith Haring, New York

170
Keith Haring
Untitled (from "*20 Untitled Drawings*"),
1988
black ink on paper, 11 x 14"
Lent by The Estate of Keith Haring,
KHD 604/20, 7/20
© The Estate of Keith Haring, New York

171
Keith Haring
Pig, 1988
acrylic on round canvas, 120" in diameter
Lent by The Estate of Keith Haring,
KHC 58
© The Estate of Keith Haring, New York

172
Keith Haring
Funny Bunny, 1988
black felt-tip pen on paper, 14 x 11"
Lent by The Estate of Keith Haring,
KHD 605
© The Estate of Keith Haring, New York

173
Keith Haring
Dress Up Clothes, 1988
black felt-tip pen on paper, 11⅝ x 15⅜"
Lent by The Estate of Keith Haring,
KHD 320/10, 3/10
© The Estate of Keith Haring, New York

174
Keith Haring
Dress Up Clothes, 1988
black felt-tip pen on paper, 11⅝ x 15⅜"
Lent by The Estate of Keith Haring,
KHD 320/10, 5/10
© The Estate of Keith Haring, New York

175
Keith Haring
Birth Announcement, 1988
black felt-tip pen, paper collage, and
graphite on paper, 14 x 11"
Lent by The Estate of Keith Haring,
KHD 782
© The Estate of Keith Haring, New York

176
Keith Haring
Untitled (Pop Shop Billboard), 1989
black felt-tip pen on paper, 11 x 14"
Lent by The Estate of Keith Haring,
KHD 788
© The Estate of Keith Haring, New York

177
Keith Haring
Billboard Design, 1989
black felt-tip pen on paper, 14 x 17"
Lent by The Estate of Keith Haring,
KHD 758
© The Estate of Keith Haring, New York

178
Keith Haring
Self-Portrait from a *Portfolio of 8 Self-
Portraits,* 1989
black ink on paper, 15 x 10⅞"
Lent by The Estate of Keith Haring,
KHD 271/8, 1/8
© The Estate of Keith Haring, New York

179
Keith Haring
Logo Against Family Violence, 1989
black felt-tip pen on paper, 14 x 8½"
Lent by The Estate of Keith Haring,
KHD 538
© The Estate of Keith Haring, New York

180
Keith Haring
Act Up For Life, 1989
black felt-tip pen on paper, 9⅛ x 8⅝"
Lent by The Estate of Keith Haring,
KHD 546
© The Estate of Keith Haring, New York

181
Keith Haring
AIDS Poster – Vienna, 1989
black felt-tip pen, paper collage, and tape
on paper, 14 x 11"
Lent by The Estate of Keith Haring,
KHD 557
© The Estate of Keith Haring, New York

182
Keith Haring
Untitled, 1989
acrylic and enamel on canvas, 73 x 73"
Lent by The Estate of Keith Haring,
KHC 43
© The Estate of Keith Haring, New York

183
Keith Haring
Lil' Angel Design, 1989
black felt-tip pen on paper, 9¼ x 9⅛"
Lent by The Estate of Keith Haring,
KHD 556
© The Estate of Keith Haring, New York

184
Keith Haring
*Untitled (Drawing for Pyramid
Sculpture),* 1990
black ink on board, 38½ x 60"
Lent by The Estate of Keith Haring,
KHD 719/4, 1/4
© The Estate of Keith Haring, New York

185
Keith Haring
*Untitled (Drawing for Pyramid
Sculpture),* 1990
black ink on board, 38½ x 60"
Lent by The Estate of Keith Haring,
KHD 719/4, 2/4
© The Estate of Keith Haring, New York

186
Keith Haring
*Untitled (Drawing for Pyramid
Sculpture),* 1990
black ink on board, 38½ x 60"
Lent by The Estate of Keith Haring,
KHD 719/4, 3/4
© The Estate of Keith Haring, New York

187
Keith Haring
*Untitled (Drawing for Pyramid
Sculpture),* 1990
black ink on board, 38½ x 60"
Lent by The Estate of Keith Haring,
KHD 719/4, 4/4
© The Estate of Keith Haring, New York

188
* Keith Haring
Pyramid, 1991
painted aluminum, 27½ x 55 x 55"
Lent by The Estate of Keith Haring, KHS
© The Estate of Keith Haring, New York

189
Keith Haring
Pop Shop Tokyo, not dated
black felt-tip pen on paper, 21¼ x 15¼"
Lent by The Estate of Keith Haring,
KHD 15
© The Estate of Keith Haring, New York

225

190
Keith Haring
Pop Shop, not dated
black felt-tip pen and sticker on paper,
23 x 29″
Lent by The Estate of Keith Haring,
KHD 502
© The Estate of Keith Haring, New York

191
Keith Haring
Pop Shop Bag, not dated
silkscreen on plastic, 19 x 16¾″
Lent by The Estate of Keith Haring
© The Estate of Keith Haring, New York

192
Keith Haring
Untitled, not dated
black felt-tip pen on paper, 13⅞ x 16⅞″
Lent by The Estate of Keith Haring,
KHD 693
© The Estate of Keith Haring, New York

193
Keith Haring
Untitled (from *"20 Untitled Drawings"*),
not dated
black felt-tip pen on paper, 11 x 11⅛″
Lent by The Estate of Keith Haring,
KHD 831/20, 5/20
© The Estate of Keith Haring, New York

194
Keith Haring
Radiant Child from the *Artist's Sketch-
book (Babies, Dogs, etc.),* not dated
black felt-tip pen on paper, 14 x 17″
Lent by The Estate of Keith Haring,
KHD 944/21, 12/21
© The Estate of Keith Haring, New York

195
Keith Haring
*Block Head, Cat Hat, Whassup?,
Chilly Willy, Dancy Nancy, Lil' Angel,
Funny Bunny,* not dated T-shirts
Lent by The Estate of Keith Haring
© The Estate of Keith Haring, New York

* In the Phoenix Art Museum venue only
** Not in the Phoenix Art Museum venue

Biographies

Walt Disney

1901 Born December 5 in Chicago.

1918 Attempted to enlist for military service but was refused because of his age. Joined the Red Cross instead and went overseas for a year. Drove an ambulance which he covered with drawings and cartoons.

1920 Returned to US, to Kansas City, and began his career as an advertising cartoonist. Created and marketed his first original animated cartoons.

1923 Moved to Hollywood with a completed animation and live-action film. With his brother and their combined savings of $290 plus $500 borrowed from an uncle, he set up a production company and they created the first "Alice Comedy" featurette.

1924 Ceased doing any of the actual drawing for his animations. Began concentrating on production and development of the business.

1925 Married Lillian Bounds (they had two children).

1928 Conceived the idea of Mickey Mouse during a long train ride from New York to Los Angeles. Mickey starred in *Steamboat Willie*, the world's first fully synchronized sound cartoon.

1930s Introduced such characters as Goofy, Pluto, Donald Duck, Minnie Mouse, the Three Little Pigs and the Big Bad Wolf. Began merchandising Disney characters in the early 1930s.

1932 Technicolor was introduced during the production of his *Silly Symphonies*. The film *Flowers and Trees* won the first of 32 personal Academy Awards. Received a special award from the the Academy of Motion Picture Arts and Sciences for the creation of Mickey Mouse. Altogether, Disney and his company received 48 Academy Awards and 7 Emmys in his lifetime.

1933 Completed *Three Little Pigs* in color. Disney now employed over 100 people.

1934 Began production of *Snow White and the Seven Dwarfs*, the first feature-length animated cartoon ever made. It cost $1.5 million and took three years to make.

1935 Received the French Legion of Honor for "creating a new art form in which good will is spread throughout the world." First Mickey Mouse cartoon in color.

1937 Released *The Old Mill*, the first short subject to use the multiplane camera technique. Premiered *Snow White and the Seven Dwarfs*.

1938 Produced *Brave Little Tailor* and *Ferdinand the Bull*.

1940 Released *Pinocchio* and *Fantasia*. Construction was completed on Disney's Burbank studio. Did special government work during World War II.

1941 Released *Dumbo*. Began to make instructional films for the armed services.

1942 *Bambi*

1945 Released the musical *The Three Caballeros*, combining live action with cartoons, a process also used in *Song of the South* and *Mary Poppins*.

1950 Released *Cinderella*. Completed his first feature-length live action film, *Treasure Island*. On Christmas Day, showed his favorite cartoon characters on television for the first time.

1951 *Alice in Wonderland*

1953 *Peter Pan*

1955 *Disneyland* opens. A total of 250 million people had visited it by 1985. Began broadcasting *The Mickey Mouse Club* on television.

1959 *Sleeping Beauty*

1961 Was one of the first to present full color television programming with *Wonderful World of Color*.

1965 Announced the "Florida Project" which became Walt Disney World.

1966 Launched the design for the Experimental Prototype Community of Tomorrow, or EPCOT. Died on December 15. Eighty-one features were released during his lifetime.

Andy Warhol

1928 Born Andrew Warhola August 6 in Pittsburgh.

1945–49 Majored in pictorial design at the Carnegie Institute of Technology, Pittsburgh.

1949 Moved to New York City. Began to use the name "Warhol" instead of "Warhola."

1952 First solo exhibition at the Hugo Gallery, New York, titled *Andy Warhol: Fifteen Drawings Based on the Writings of Truman Capote.*

1953 Published promotional books in collaboration with Ralph Ward, *A is an Alphabet, There was Snow on the Street and Rain in the Sky,* and *Love is a Pink Cake.*

1956 Participated in his first group exhibition held at the Museum of Modern Art: *Recent Drawings USA*

1956+59 Solo exhibitions at Bodley Gallery, New York.

1960 Made his first Pop Art images and paintings of the comic strip characters *Batman, Dick Tracy, Nancy, Saturday's Popeye,* and *Superman.*

1962 Painted the first *Campbell's Soup Cans* and showed them at the Ferus Gallery in Los Angeles. *Warren* and *Troy* are among the first silkscreens. Silkscreened the first Marilyns, Elvises, and Disasters. Solo show at the Stable Gallery, New York City. Included in an important Pop Art group exhibition – *The New Realists* at the Sidney Janis Gallery, New York.

1963 Bought a 16mm movie camera and shot his first films, including *Sleep* and *Eat.* Used a Polaroid camera for the first time. Moved his studio into a firehouse which became know as "The Factory." Silkscreened the Electric Chairs and Race Riots.

1964 Ileana Sonnabend Gallery hosted his first solo show in Europe. Solo show at Leo Castelli Gallery, New York. Received mural commission for the New York State Pavilion at the New York World's Fair which was censored and painted over. Made the films *Empire, Harlot,* and *The Thirteen Most Beautiful Women.*

1965 First solo museum exhibition at the Institute of Contemporary Art, University of Pennsylvania. Met Paul Morrisey, who became important to film production with Warhol at The Factory. Announced his retirement from painting to pursue film-making. Made the films *Vinyl, Suicide, The Life of Juanita Castro, Restaurant, My Hustler,* and *Kitchen.*

1966 Made the film *The Chelsea Girls* which became the first underground film to be shown in a commercial theater. Began to produce multi-media presentations. Rented the Dom for a month and transformed it into a discotheque. Started frequenting the bar/restaurant Max's Kansas City. Accompanied the *Velvet Underground* on a concert tour.

1967 Silkscreened the Electric Chairs. Lectured at colleges in Los Angeles but quit the tour because he did not like it. Moved The Factory to Union Square. Produced the *Velvet Underground's* first album and designed its cover, a banana-skin sticker that peels off to reveal a flesh-colored banana underneath.

1968 First solo European museum exhibition at Moderna Museet, Stockholm. Filmed *Flesh.* Was shot by Valerie Solanis; spent two months in hospital.

1969 Published first issue of *Interview,* a Warhol Enterprises, Inc. magazine. Filmed *Trash.*

1970 Solo show at the Pasadena Art Museum travels to the Museum of Contemporary Art, Chicago; Stedelijk Van Abbemuseum, Eindhoven, The Netherlands; Musée d'Art Moderne de la Ville de Paris; Tate Gallery, London; and Whitney Museum of American Art, New York.

1971 *Pork,* a Warhol play, was performed in London and New York.

1972 Renewed his focus on painting. Began painting commissioned portraits. Until his death he painted 50–100 a year. Eventually, Mick Jagger, Princess Caroline, Sylvester Stallone, Truman Capote, the Shah of Iran, and Keith Haring were his subjects.

1973 Acted in the film *The Driver's Seat,* with Elizabeth Taylor.

1974 Moved his studio to Broadway.

1975 Harcourt Brace Jovanovich published *The Philosophy of Andy Warhol (from A to B and Back Again).*

1976–79 Silkscreened the *Skulls, Athletes, Hammer and Sickles, Torsos, Oxidations,* and *Shadows.* Published *Andy Warhol's Exposures,* a book of photographs. The Whitney Museum of American Art showed *Andy Warhol: Portraits of the 70s* in 1979.

1980–82 Hosted and produced "Andy Warhol Television" on cable television in New York. Harcourt Brace Jovanovich published *POPism: the Warhol '60s* in 1980.

1983 Met Keith Haring.

1984–87 Collaborated with Jean-Michel Basquiat and Francesco Clemente on paintings. Harper & Row published *America* by Andy Warhol in 1985. Showed *Andy Warhol Fifteen Minutes,* a series of short segments of celebrity guests, on MTV.

1987 Died on February 22 at a New York hospital following gall bladder surgery. Memorial service held April 1 at St. Patrick's Cathedral, New York.

Keith Haring

1958   Born May 4 in Kutztown, Pennsylvania

1976–78   Moved to Pittsburgh. Briefly studied at a commercial art school. Saw a retrospective of Pierre Alechinsky's paintings at the Carnegie Museum. Had first solo show, of abstract drawings at the Pittsburgh Center for the Arts.

1978–79   Moved to New York City and studied at the School of Visual Arts. Painted on large-scale photo backdrop paper in a street-level studio on Twenty-Second Street where he enjoyed the comments of passers-by. Videotaped the painting process.

1980   Organized exhibitions and performed at Club 57, in the basement of a church at 57 Saint Mark's Place. Participated in the *Times Square Show,* an important exhibition of new art held in New York City. Made the first drawings with flying saucers, animal, and human images that recur in the subway drawings.

1981   Made the first white chalk drawings on the black paper pasted over expired advertisements in New York City's subway stations. Painted on plastic, metal, found objects, and garden statuary. Curated exhibitions of drawings and graffiti art at the Mudd Club. Solo show at Club 57. Participated in the *New York/New Wave* show in New York. Painted first mural in a schoolyard on the Lower East Side. Met the graffiti artist L.A. II (Angel Ortiz).

1982   Collaborated with L.A. II. Began painting on tarpaulins. First solo gallery exhibition at Tony Shafrazi Gallery. Participated in *Documenta* 7 in Kassel, West Germany. Drew a thirty-second animation for the *Spectacolor Billboard* in Times Square which ran continuously for a month.

1983   Participated in the Whitney Biennial and the São Paulo Bienal. Showed collaborations with graffiti artist L.A. II at Fun Gallery, New York; Robert Fraser Gallery, London; and Galerie Watari, Tokyo. Second exhibition at Tony Shafrazi Gallery. Met Andy Warhol.

1984   Painted murals in Sydney, Melbourne, Rio de Janeiro, Dobbs Ferry, Minneapolis, and Manhattan. Created sixty-second animated commercial for *Big,* a store in Zurich, Switzerland.

1985   Began painting on canvas. Simultaneously exhibited paintings at Tony Shafrazi Gallery and brightly colored painted steel sculptures at Leo Castelli Gallery. Solo exhibition at the Musée d'Art Contemporain, Bordeaux. Participated in the Paris Biennial. Designed sets for *Sweet Saturday Night,* Brooklyn Academy of Music, New York, and *The Marriage of Heaven and Hell,* for the Ballet National de Marseille, France. Painted 25 x 32-foot backdrop for *The Palladium,* New York City. Printed and distributed 20,000 *Free South Africa* posters. Designed four watches for *Swatch Watch USA.*

1986   Stopped doing subway drawings. Solo exhibition at the Stedelijk Museum, Amsterdam. Three large-scale sculptures temporarily installed at Hammarskjold Plaza, New York City. Opened the Pop Shop, a store selling Haring products and multiples. Painted the *Crack is Wack* mural as well as outdoor murals on the Berlin Wall and in Amsterdam, Paris, and Phoenix, Arizona. Body-painted Grace Jones for her video *I'm Not Perfect.* Collaborated with Brion Gysin on *Fault Lines* and Jenny Holzer on billboards for *Vienna Festival '86.*

1987   Solo shows in Helsinki, Antwerp, and Knokke, Belgium. Showed painted steel masks and paintings on canvas at Tony Shafrazi Gallery. Participated in *Art Against AIDS,* a benefit exhibition curated by Steven Reichard. Painted murals in Düsseldorf, Paris, Antwerp, New York, and Knokke. Designed street signs for Tokyo.

1988   Opened the Pop Shop in Tokyo. Painted murals in Chicago and Atlanta with children and conducted workshops. Painted *Easter at the White House* mural erected on the White House lawn, then donated to the Children's Hospital, Washington, D.C. Painted mural at FDR Drive and Houston Street in Manhattan. Showed at the Hans Mayer Gallery, Düsseldorf, and Tony Shafrazi Gallery.

1989   Engaged in widespread campaign for AIDS awareness. Painted murals in Monaco, Chicago, New York, Iowa City, and on the exterior wall of a monastery in Pisa. Established the Keith Haring Foundation, a charitable organization seeking to contribute to a wide range of social concerns. Showed at Gallery 121, Antwerp.

1990   Died of AIDS on February 16.

Selected Bibliographies

Walt Disney

Bailey, Adrian, *Walt Disney's World of Fantasy*. New York: Gallery Books, 1987.

Bain, David, and Bruce Harris, *Mickey Mouse: Fifty Happy Years*. New York: Harmony Books, 1977.

Beard, Richard R., *Walt Disney's Epcot Center*. New York: Harry N. Abrams, 1982.

Birnbaum, Steve, *Steve Birnbaum Brings You the Best of Walt Disney World*. Boston, Massachusetts: Houghton Mifflin, 1981.

—, *Steve Birnbaum Brings You the Best of Disneyland*. Boston, Massachusetts: Houghton Mifflin, 1982.

Blitz, Martha, *Donald Duck*. New York: Harmony Books, 1979.

Bright, Randy, *Disneyland: Inside Story*. New York: Harry N. Abrams, 1987.

Culhane, John, *Fantasia*. New York: Harry N. Abrams, 1983.

"Disney Without Walt," *Forbes* (July 1, 1967), pp. 39–41.

Feild, Robert Durant, *The Art of Walt Disney*. London: Collins, 1947.

Finch, Christopher, *The Art of Walt Disney: From Mickey Mouse to the Magic Kingdoms*. New York: Harry N. Abrams, 1973.

—, *Walt Disney's America*. New York: Abbeville Press, 1978.

Fisher, Maxine, *Walt Disney*. New York: F. Watts, 1988.

Garraty, John A., and Mark C. Carnes (eds.), *Dictionary of American Biography*. New York: Charles Scribner's Sons, 1988.

Grant, John, *Encyclopedia of Walt Disney's Animated Characters*. New York: Harper & Row, 1987.

Greene, Katherine and Richard, *The Man Behind the Magic: The Story of Walt Disney*. New York: Viking, 1991.

Hillier, Bevis, and Bernard C. Shine, *Mickey Mouse Memorabilia*. New York: Abrams, 1986.

Hollis, Richard, and Brian Sibley, *Mickey Mouse, His Life and Times*. New York: Harper & Row, 1986.

Keller, Keith, *The Mickey Mouse Club Scrapbook*. New York: Grosset & Dunlap, 1975.

Kinney, Jack, *Walt Disney and Assorted Other Characters*. New York: Harmony, 1988.

Kurland, Gerald, *Walt Disney, the Master of Animation*. Charlotteville, New York: SamHar Press, 1971.

Leebron, Elizabeth, *Walt Disney: A Guide to References and Resources*. Boston: G.K. Hall, 1979.

Maltin, Leonard, *The Disney Films*. New York: Crown, 1973.

Miller, Diane Disney, and Pete Martin, *The Story of Walt Disney*. New York: Holt, 1957.

Morgenstem, J., "Walt Disney (1901–1966) Imagineer of Fun," *Newsweek* (December 26, 1966), pp. 68–9.

Mosley, Leonard, *Disney's World: A Biography*. New York: Stein & Day, 1985.

O'Brien, Flora, *Goofy the Good Sport*. New York: HP Books, 1985.

Parry-Crooke, Charlotte, and Judith Schuler, *Donald Duck: 50 Years of Happy Frustration*. New York: HP Books, 1984.

Schickel, Richard, *The Disney Version: The Life, Times, Art and Commerce of Walt Disney*. New York: Simon & Shuster, 1985.

Shale, Richard, *Donald Duck Joins Up*. Ann Arbor, Michigan: UMI Research Press, 1982.

"Silver Anniversary for Walt and Mickey," *Life* (November 2, 1953), pp. 82–90.

Taylor, John, *Storming the Magic Kingdom: How Corporate Raiders Forced a Revolution at Disney*. New York: Knopf, 1987.

Thomas, Bob, *Walt Disney: An American Original*. New York: Simon & Schuster, 1978.

—, *Walt Disney, the Art of Animation: The Story of the Disney Studio Contribution to a New Art*. New York: Simon & Schuster, 1958.

Thomas, Frank, *Disney Animation: The Illusion of Life*. New York: Abbeville Press, 1981.

—, and Ollie Johnston, *Too Funny for Words: Disney's Greatest Sight Gags*. New York: Abbeville Press, 1987.

Tumbusch, Tom, *Disneyana Catalog and Price Guide*. Dayton, Ohio: Tomart, 1985–89.

Walt Disney Productions, *Treasures of Disney Animation Art*. New York: Abbeville Press, 1982.

Andy Warhol

Amayo, Mario, *Pop Art... and After,* New York: Viking, 1966

Andy Warhol: Death and Disasters. Houston: Menil Collection and Houston Fine Arts Press, 1988.

Andy Warhol: Guns, Knives, Crosses. Madrid: Galerie Fernando Vijande, 1982.

Bailey, David, *Andy Warhol: Transcript of David Bailey's ATV Documentary.* London: Bailey Litchfield/Mathews Miller Dunbar Ltd, 1972.

Bastian, Heiner, *Joseph Beuys, Robert Rauschenberg, Cy Twombly, Andy Warhol: Sammlung Marx.* Munich: Prestel-Verlag, 1982.

Bergin, Paul, "Andy Warhol: The Artist as Machine," *Art Journal* (Summer 1967), pp. 359–63.

Billeter, Erika (ed.), *Andy Warhol: Ein Buch zur Ausstellung 1978 im Kunsthaus Zürich.* Zurich: Kunsthaus, 1978.

Bockris, Victor, *The Life and Death of Andy Warhol.* New York: Bantam Books, 1989.

Bourdon, David, *Warhol.* New York: Abrams, 1989.

Brown, Andreas, *Andy Warhol: His Early Works, 1947–1959.* New York: Gotham Book Mart, 1971.

Collaborations: Jean-Michel Basquiat, Francesco Clemente, Andy Warhol. Kusnacht/Zurich: Edition Galerie Bruno Bischofberger, 1984.

Coplans, John, Jonas Mekas and Calvin Tomkins, *Andy Warhol.* Greenwich, Connecticut: New York Graphic Society, 1970.

Crone, Rainer, *Andy Warhol.* London: Thames & Hudson, 1970.

—, *Andy Warhol: A Picture Shop by the Artist.* New York: Rizzoli, 1987.

De Salvo, Donna M. (ed.), *Success is a Job in New York... The Early Art and Business of Andy Warhol.* New York and Pittsburgh: The Grey Art Gallery and Study Center, New York University, and The Carnegie Museum of Art, 1989.

Ehrenstein, David, "Interview with Andy Warhol," *Film Culture* (Spring 1966), p. 41.

Fairbrother, Trevor, "Warhol Meets Sargent at the Whitney," *Arts Magazine* (February 1987).

Finch, Christopher, *Pop Art; Object and Image.* London: Studio Vista, and New York: Dutton in association with the Metropolitan Museum of Art, 1969.

Geldzahler, Henry, *Andy Warhol.* Bogota: Galerie Fernando Quintant, 1988.

—, *Andy Warhol: A Memorial.* New York: Dia Art Foundation, 1987.

—, *Pop Art, 1955–70.* Sydney: International Cultural Corporation of Australia Ltd, 1985.

Green, Samuel Adams, *Andy Warhol.* Philadelphia: Institute of Contemporary Art, University of Pennsylvania, 1965.

Haskell, Barbara, *Blam! The Explosion of Pop, Minimalism, and Performance 1958–64.* New York: Whitney Mueum of American Art in association with W.W. Norton, 1984.

Koch, Stephen, *Andy Warhol Photographs.* New York: Robert Miller Gallery, 1986.

—, *Stargazer: Andy Warhol and His Films.* New York: Praeger, 1973.

Licht, Ira, *Andy Warhol: Ten Portraits of Jews of the Twentieth Century.* Coral Gables, Florida: Lowe Art Museum, University of Miami, 1980.

McShine, Kynaston (ed.), *Andy Warhol: A Retrospective.* New York: Museum of Modern Art, 1989.

Pomeroy, Ralph, "An Interview with Andy Warhol, June, 1970," *Afterimage* (Fall 1970), pp. 34–9.

Ratcliff, Carter, *Andy Warhol.* New York: Abbeville Press, 1983.

Schjeldahl, Peter, "Warhol and Class Content," *Art in America* (May 1980).

Smith, Patrick S., *Andy Warhol's Art and Films.* Ann Arbor: UMI Research Press, 1986.

Solomon, Alan, *Andy Warhol.* Boston: Institute of Contemporary Art, 1966.

Stanton, Suzy, "On Warhol's *Campbell's Soup Can,*" in *Andy Warhol.* New York: Stable Gallery, 1962.

Swenson, G.R., "What is Pop Art? Answers from 8 Painters, Part I," *Art News* (November 1963).

Taylor, Paul, "Andy Warhol: The Last Interview," *Flash Art* (April 1987), pp. 40–4.

Warhol, Andy, *25 Cats Named Sam and One Blue Pussy.* New York: printed by Seymour Berlin, 1954.

—, *A la Recherche du Shoe Perdu,* New York: Warhol, 1955.

—, *America.* New York: Harper & Row, 1985.

—, Kaspar König, Pontus Hulten and Olle Granath (eds.), *Andy Warhol.* Stockholm: Moderna Museet, 1968.

—, *Andy Warhol's Index (Book),* New York: Random House, 1967.

—, with Ralph T. Ward, *Love is a Pink Cake.* New York: Warhol, 1953.

—, *The Philosophy of Andy Warhol (From A to B and Back Again).* New York: Harcourt Brace Jovanovich, 1975.

—, and Pat Hackett, *POPism: The Warhol '60s.* New York: Harcourt Brace Jovanovich, 1980.

Wilcock, John, *The Autobiography and Sex Life of Andy Warhol.* New York: Other Scenes, 1971.

Keith Haring

Adams, Brook, "Keith Haring: Subways are for Drawing," *Print Collector's Newsletter* (May/June 1982), Vol. 13, p. 45.

Alinovi, Francesca, "Twenty-first Century Slang: Keith Haring, Interview with the Artist," *Flash Art* (November 1983), No. 114, pp. 23–31.

Blinder, Martin, and Dan Cameron, *Keith Haring 1988*. Van Nuys, California: Martin Lawrence Limited Editions, 1988.

Blinderman, Barry, "Keith Haring's Subterranean Signatures," *Arts Magazine* (September 1981), Vol. 56, pp. 104–5.

Burroughs, William, Barry Blinderman, Timothy Leary, Maarten van de Guchte and Vince Aletti, *Keith Haring: Future Primeval*. Normal, Illinois: University of Illinois, 1990.

Castelli, Leo, *Beyond the Canvas*. New York: Rizzoli International Publications, 1985.

Deitch, Jeffrey, *Keith Haring: Painting, Drawings and a Vellum*. Amsterdam: Stedelijk Museum, 1986.

Dickhoff, Wilfried (ed.), *What It Is*. New York: Tony Shafrazi Gallery, 1986.

Drenger, Daniel, "Art and Life: An Interview with Keith Haring," *Columbia Law Review* (Spring 1988), pp. 44–53.

Fox, Howard N., *Avant-Garde in the Eighties*. Los Angeles: Los Angeles County Museum of Art, 1987.

Frackman, N., and R. Kaufman, "Documenta 7: The Dialogue and a Few Asides," *Arts Magazine* (October 1982), Vol. 57, pp. 91–7.

Froment, Jean-Louis, Brion Gysin and Sylvie Couderc, *Keith Haring: Peintures, Sculptures et Dessins*. Bordeaux: Musée d'Art Contemporain de Bordeaux, 1985.

Gablik, Suzi, "Report from New York: The Graffiti Question," *Art in America* (October 1982), Vol. 70, pp. 33–7.

Galloway, David, "Keith Haring: Made in Germany," *Art in America* (March 1991), Vol. 79, pp. 118–23.

—, *Keith Haring: 1983*. Paris: La Galerie de Poche, 1990.

Geldzahler, Henry, and Keith Haring, *Art in Transit*. New York: Harmony Books, 1984.

Gruen, John, *Keith Haring: The Authorized Biography*. New York: Prentice-Hall, 1991.

Hager, Steven, *Hip-Hop*. New York: St. Martin's Press, 1984.

Haring, Keith, *against all odds*. Rotterdam, Holland: Bebert, 1990.

—, *Eight Ball*. Kyoto, Japan: Kyoto Shein International, 1989.

Honnef, Klaus, *Back to the USA*. Bonn: Rheinisches Landesmuseum und Rheinland-Verlag, 1982.

Keith Haring: A Memorial Exhibition. New York: Tony Shafrazi Gallery, 1990.

Kuspit, Donald, "Haring at Tony Shafrazi and Leo Castelli," *Artforum* (February 1986), Vol. 24, pp. 102–3.

Linker, Kate, "Keith Haring," *Artforum* (March 1984).

Marzorati, Gerald, "Signs of the Times," *Soho News* (May 13, 1981).

McCormack, Ed, "Pop Goes the Easel," *Daily News Magazine* (August 4, 1985).

McGill, Douglas, "Art People," *New York Times* (November 8, 1985), p. C 33.

Pailhas, Roger, Jean-Louis Marcos and Marcellin Pleynet, *New York '85*. Marseilles: ARCA Centre d'Art Contemporain.

Pincus-Witten, Robert, Jeffrey Deitch and David Shapiro, *Keith Haring,* New York: Tony Shafrazi Gallery, 1982.

Reynard, Delphine, "Graffiti-writers, Graffiti-artists," *Art Press* (May 1984).

Ricard, Rene, "The Radiant Child," *Artforum* (December 1981), Vol. 20, pp. 35–43.

Rosenzweig, Phyllis, Howard Fox and Miranda McClintic, *Content: A Contemporary Focus 1974–1984*. Washington, D.C.: Smithsonian Institution, 1984.

Rubell, Jason, "Keith Haring: The Last Interview," *Arts Magazine* (September 1990), Vol. 65, pp. 52–9.

Rubin, William (ed.), *Primitivism in 20th Century Art*. New York: Museum of Modern Art, 1984.

Small, Michael, "Drawing on Walls, Clothes, and Subways, Keith Haring Earns Favor with Art Lovers High and Low," *People* (December 5, 1983), Vol. 20, p. 147.

Smith, Roberta, "Critical Dealings," *The Village Voice* (September 13, 1983).

Sonne, Nikolaus, and Christian Holzfuss, *Subway Drawings*. Berlin: Galerie Nikolaus Sonne, 1990.

Span, Paula, "Subway to Museums: Graffiti's Scrawl of Success," *Washington Post* (December 30, 1985), Section D, pp. 1–2.

Foreword

1 Andy Warhol and Pat Hacket, *POPism: the Warhol '60s*, New York and London: Harcourt Brace Jovanovich, 1980, p. 186.

Keith Haring, Andy Warhol, and Walt Disney

1 Andy Warhol, Kaspar König, Pontus Hulten, and Olle Granath (eds), *Andy Warhol*, Stockholm: Moderna Museet, 1968, not paginated.
2 Trevor J. Fairbrother, "Warhol meets Sargent at the Whitney," *Arts Magazine*, February 1987, p. 70.
3 Daniel Drenger, "Art and Life: An Interview with Keith Haring," *Columbia Art Review*, Spring 1988, p. 46.
4 John Updike, "The Mystery of Mickey Mouse," *Art and Antiques*, November 1991, p. 64.
5 Peter Schjeldahl, "Warhol and Class Content," *Art in America*, May 1980, p. 117.
6 They are called "cels" because they used to be painted on cellulose nitrate, the same material used as a backing for the emulsion of early films. In mid-1940, cellulose nitrate was replaced with an acetate material. From 1938–46, the Disney Company had an arrangement through the Courvoisier Galleries in San Francisco to sell animation art. Many cels from Disney's earliest films were sold this way, most of them overlaid on backgrounds authorized by Disney but not actually used in a film. These are called "Courvoisier cel setups." Also, cels were washed and re-used during the war years since plastic was then scarce. Many cels were sold in the Disney Art Corner at Disneyland after it opened in 1955.
7 Updike, *op. cit.*, p. 65.
8 G.R. Swenson, "What is Pop Art?: Answers from 8 Painters, Part I," *Art News* 62, November 1963, p. 26.
9 While untraditional, Warhol's practice was not entirely unheard of. For example, Peter Paul Rubens (1577–1640) and other seventeenth-century masters employed assistants to paint significant portions of their large canvases, as did many subsequent artists such as the French painter Jacques Louis David (1749–1825). The French sculptor Auguste Rodin (1840–1917) had large numbers of the same sculptural design produced by studio assistants in various sizes and media, causing him to be referred to as "the Henry Ford of sculpture" in homage to the American automobile manufacturer who perfected the assembly line, leading to the mass production of relatively inexpensive automobiles.
10 Read by Nicholas Love at the Memorial

Mass for Andy Warhol, Saint Patrick's Cathedral, New York, April 1, 1987.
11 Warhol, König, et al., *op. cit.*
12 James A. Revson, "Haring's Gift: Gifts," *Newsday*, April 18, 1986, Part II, p. 3.
13 Suzanne Slesin, "An Artist Turns Retailer," *New York Times*, April 18, 1986, Section 1, p. 22.
14 John Gruen, *Keith Haring: The Authorized Biography*, New York: Prentice-Hall, 1991, p. 148.
15 Drenger, *op. cit.*, p. 52.
16 Gruen, *op. cit.*, p. 142.
17 Drenger, *op. cit.*, p. 46.
18 Warhol, König, et al., *op. cit.*
19 Gretchen Berg, "Andy: My True Story," *Los Angeles Free Press*, March 17, 1967, p. 3 (reprinted from *East Village Other*).
20 *Ibid.*
21 Gruen, *op. cit.*, p. 169.

Disney in Context

1 The Disney archives contain bulging files of Horvath's work from the 1930s, most of them for cartoon projects that were subsequently abandoned.
2 The term "one-sheet" denotes a movie poster usually printed on a single large 27 x 41" sheet; the Disney studio would later use three-sheet and six-sheet posters to promote its feature films. These giant advertisements, printed in several overlapping pieces, would be pasted like wallpaper onto boards; hence few survive. See catalogue number 66, a three-sheet for the 1950s re-release of *Snow White and the Seven Dwarfs*.
3 Thomas Andrae, "Of Mouse and the Man: Floyd Gottfredson and the Mickey Mouse Continuities," in *Mickey Mouse in Color*, Prescott, Arizona: Another Rainbow Publishing Company, Inc., 1988, pp. 12–15.
4 The small ink drawings paired with the posters for *Donald's Cousin Gus* and *Beach Picnic* (catalogue numbers 50 and 46) are not the originals to the one-sheets, though at first glance they appear to be. The finished art for stone lithographs such as these posters must be etched directly onto the plates from which they are printed. Thus the artist of record is actually the engraver; but he must have something from which to work. It is believed that these drawings were provided to guide him; perhaps the images were enlarged and traced onto the plates. Some details differ between the pen drawings and the finished posters, most notably in the line weight.
5 See Frank Thomas and Ollie Johnston, *Disney Animation: The Illusion of Life*, New

York: Abbeville Press, 1981.
6 Geoffrey Blum, "The Greatest Escape of All," *Storyboard/The Art of Laughter*, Vol. 2, No. 2, April/May 1991, p. 29.
7 Christopher Finch, *The Art of Walt Disney: From Mickey Mouse to the Magic Kingdoms*, New York: Harry N. Abrams, 1973, pp. 182, 215.

Andy's Enterprise: Nothing Special

1 *The Philosophy of Andy Warhol (From A to B and Back Again)*, New York: Harcourt Brace Jovanovich, 1975, p. 62.
2 *POPism: The Warhol '60s*, New York: Harcout Brace Jovanovich, 1980, p. 4.
3 Yvor Winters' opening remark to his poetry seminars at Stanford University during the 1950s and 1960s. Gus Blaisdell, Albuquerque, New Mexico.
4 John Brown, *An Estimate of Manners and Principles of the Times*, 2nd edn, 1757, p. 58.
5 Balcomb Greene, "Expression as Production," catalogue of an exhibition, *American Abstract Artists*, Section XI, New York, 1938, not paginated.
6 Portions of the material in the following two sections of this essay appeared in a different form in my short critical memoir of Warhol and the 1960s entitled "Getting It Exactly Wrong: Andy's Kindergarten for Connoisseurs," *Parkett Magazine*, No. 20, Zurich, 1989, pp. 160–3.
7 *Philosophy of Andy Warhol*, p. 158.
8 Read by Nicholas Love at the Memorial Mass for Andy Warhol, Saint Patrick's Cathedral, New York, April 1, 1987.
9 *POPism*, p. 287.
10 Quoted in G.R. Swenson, "What is Pop Art?: Answers from 8 Painters, Part I," *Art News* 62, November 1963, p. 26.
11 Quoted by Edmund White, from "A Collective Portrait of Andy Warhol," in *Andy Warhol: A Retrospective*, New York: The Museum of Modern Art, 1989, p. 441.
12 Since I was always the guy who got to exclaim, *"Where's the soup?"* and since I have not seen this little piece of street wisdom published elsewhere, I offer it on my own authority. Also, I should note here that street exegesis of Warhol's images was not uncommon during the 1960s. They were, I think, a natural offshoot of amphetamine culture. I remember a dazed speed queen explaining to me at Max's one night that the allusion of the soup cans was to Frank Campbell's – the funeral home of the stars – that the cans were little coffins (get it?) filled with Andy's blood. This reading, I think, needs to be taken with a few

grains of methadrine.

[13] *POPism,* p. 3.

[14] Barbara Rose, "Pop Art at the Guggenheim," *Art International* 2, 1963, pp. 20–2.

[15] *POPism,* p. 40.

[16] *Philosophy of Andy Warhol,* pp. 82–3.

[17] *POPism,* pp. 36–7.

[18] *Philosophy of Andy Warhol,* p. 96.

[19] *POPism,* p. 16.

[20] *Ibid.,* pp. 17–18.

[21] *Ibid.,* p. 263.

[22] *Philosophy of Andy Warhol,* p. 99.

[23] *POPism,* p. 16.

The Radiant Child (Keith Haring)

[1] Rene Ricard, "The Radiant Child," *Artforum,* December 1981, p. 36.

[2] Ed McCormack, "Pop Goes the Easel," *Daily News Magazine,* August 4, 1985, p. 21.

[3] Jason Rubell, "Keith Haring: The Last Interview," *Arts Magazine,* September 1990, p. 59.

[4] David Galloway, "Keith Haring: Made in Germany," *Art in America,* March 1991, p. 163.

[5] After Haring moved to New York City in 1978, he gave performances at the Club 57, located in the basement of a church at 57 Saint Mark's Place.

[6] Daniel Drenger, "Art and Life: An Interview with Keith Haring," *Columbia Art Review,* Spring 1988, p. 48.

[7] Paula Span, "Subway to Museums: Graffiti's Scrawl of Success," *Washington Post,* December 30, 1985, p. D 2.

[8] Because showing the subway drawings in the context of an art museum is contrary to the context in which Haring intended them to be seen, we have not included any in our exhibition. Many were recently shown in *Future Primeval,* a touring show organized by Barry Blinderman for the University Art Gallery, University of Illinois at Normal.

[9] Keith Haring, *Flash Art,* March 1984, p. 24.

[10] Rubell, *op. cit.,* p. 58.

[11] *Ibid.,* p. 55.

[12] Keith Haring, *against all odds,* Rotterdam, Holland: Bebert, 1990, unpaginated.

[13] John Gruen, *Keith Haring: The Authorized Biography,* New York: Prentice-Hall, 1991, p. 153.

[14] *Ibid.,* p. 85.

[15] Ambrose Vollard, *Degas,* Paris: Les Editions G. Cres & Cie, 1924, p. 112.

[16] Gruen, *op. cit.,* p. 132.

[17] *Ibid.*

[18] *Ibid.,* p. 133.

[19] Barry Blinderman, "Keith Haring's Subterranean Signatures," *Arts Magazine,* September 1981, p. 165.

[20] Drenger, *op. cit.,* p. 46.

[21] Span, *op. cit.*

[22] Galloway, *op. cit.,* p. 120.

[23] Drenger, *op. cit.,* p. 45.

[24] *Ibid.,* p. 53.

Index

Photo Credits

GL